THE FUTURE OF VIDEOTEXT

Worldwide Prospects for Home/Office Electronic Information Services

by
Efrem Sigel
with
Peter Sommer
Jeffrey Silverstein
Colin McIntyre
Blaise Downey

Knowledge Industry Publications, Inc.
White Plains, N.Y., and London

Prentice-Hall, Inc.
Englewood Cliffs, New Jersey 07632

Library of Congress Cataloging in Publication Data

Sigel, Efrem.
    The future of videotext.

    Bibliography: p.
    Includes index.
        1. Television supplies industry.   2. Computer industry.
    3. Videotex (Data transmission system)   4. Television
    display systems.   5. Market surveys.   I. Sommer, Peter.
    II. Title.
    HD9696.T462S57 1984   338.4'7621388   83-17689
    ISBN 0-13-345777-X
    ISBN 0-13-345769-9 (A Reward book : pbk.)
    ISBN 0-86729-025-0 (Knowledge Industry Publications)

© 1983 by Efrem Sigel

Printed in the United States of America.

10   9   8   7   6   5   4   3   2   1

ISBN 0-13-345777-X

ISBN 0-13-345769-9 {A REWARD BOOK : PBK.}

ISBN 0-86729-025-0

{KNOWLEDGE INDUSTRY PUBLICATIONS}

This book is available at a special discount when ordered in
bulk quantities. Contact Prentice-Hall, Inc., General
Publishing Division, Special Sales, Englewood Cliffs, N.J. 07632.

Prentice-Hall International, Inc., *London*
Prentice-Hall of Australia Pty. Limited, *Sydney*
Prentice-Hall Canada Inc., *Toronto*
Prentice-Hall of India Private Limited, *New Delhi*
Prentice-Hall of Japan, Inc., *Tokyo*
Prentice-Hall of Southeast Asia Pte. Ltd., *Singapore*
Whitehall Books Limited, *Wellington, New Zealand*
Editora Prentice-Hall do Brasil Ltda., *Rio de Janeiro*

Table of Contents

List of Tables, Figures and Appendixes

Foreword

When our first book on this subject, *Videotext: The Coming Revolution in Home/Office Information Retrieval* was published nearly three years ago, the term meant little to most people, even those involved in the world of communications. Today, the term still means little to the average consumer, but a great deal to those in publishing, broadcasting, computers and information services. Few professional writers, editors, journalists, librarians, news producers or computer engineers can afford to ignore the awesome possibilities inherent in electronic dissemination of the written word: its potential for creating or destroying jobs, changing the work place, sweeping away old habits and instilling new ones. It is out of appreciation for, even fear of, this potential that communications companies and agencies have spent hundreds of millions of dollars to create the videotext industry. That the spending is going on, that the industry exists, cannot be doubted; but it is still a curious business, one whose revenues come not from customers, but from the R&D budgets of supporting organizations. Almost all successful inventions, of course, begin in just this way: first the idea, then the need; supply creates demand. It must be noted, however, that unsuccessful inventions begin in a similar way: supply, but no demand. It sometimes takes years to know in which category an invention fits.

Today, almost everything about videotext remains uncharted and controversial—not the least being what to call it. Viewdata, teletext, TV text, cabletext, videotex (the latter more and more widely used) all have their adherents. Our own preference is still videotext. It captures the essence of the new technology—display of text on a video screen—without doing violence to established English spelling and usage. Just as every other kind of text in English has the final "t" so should it be with videotext. (It is true that "videotex" has received the sanction of various committees and international standards organizations, but when it comes to language, common sense and tradition usually win out.)

Efrem Sigel

Acknowledgments

I would like to thank some of the people and organizations who helped in the making of this book, especially Harry Smith, vice president, technology, CBS, Inc. for his generous review of the chapter on videotext technology. Karen Sirabian, associate editor, Knowledge Industry Publications, Inc. unearthed many hard-to-find statistics. Thanks are also due to the organizations who shared their information and illustrations with me: among them, Prestel, SOFRATEV, Telidon and the Federal Department of Communications (Canada), Japan's Captain system, and the Videotex Industry Association in the U.S., as well as the manufacturers who contributed photographs to this book.

Efrem Sigel

1

Introduction

by Efrem Sigel

Videotext is a means of displaying words, numbers and pictures on a TV screen at the touch of a button. The technology is simple, ingenious and potentially revolutionary; it has dozens or hundreds of applications.

Since its commercial introduction in 1976, videotext has become a metaphor for a new world of information dissemination: a world in which text and pictures are stored as electronic impulses, transmitted in seconds at the touch of a button, displayed in color in millions of homes and offices. In this metaphor, videotext stands for the future, whereas older methods of transmitting information—mainly, print on paper—represent the past. Those who develop videotext systems, or who advocate their use, do so with the unspoken conviction that the technology is an improvement over printed communications.

There are two principal versions of videotext. One, a broadcast system known as teletext, involves the one-way sending of pages of information from the TV transmitter. The amount of information is determined by the number of lines in the TV picture allocated to data transmission (typically, only a hundred or so pages can be so carried), and while the viewer can determine the timing of what he sees, teletext is not a truly interactive medium. The other version, known as viewdata or videotext or videotex, involves the sending of information from a central computer to an individual terminal over telephone lines. In this version the amount of information is unlimited—as long as the world does not run out of computer disks—and both the selection of information and the timing of its display are determined by the recipient.

Videotext had its origins in research conducted by the British Post Office (BPO) in the late 1960s and the British Broadcasting Corporation (BBC) in the early 1970s. The BPO was intrigued by the notion of an inexpensive information retrieval service that would help boost the low usage of the British telephone network. The BBC began by seeking a means of transmitting captions that would help deaf people enjoy TV programs, and in the process hit upon a data transmission service with far wider applications. Similar research was in progress at a French research center serving that nation's broadcasting and telephone industries, at a Canadian government institute and at the Japanese telephone company. By the mid to late 1970s, the systems developed by the British and French—quite similar in appearance, though different in technique—were in experimental use in those countries, as well as elsewhere in Europe, while the technically more advanced Canadian system was in full-fledged development. By 1981, teletext or viewdata trials were underway in a score of countries around the world, including the U.S. Only Britain, however, had a functioning commercial service. Figure 1.1 gives some of the history of videotext over the past 12 years.

Figure 1.1: Chronology of Videotext

1970	Sam Fedida at British Post Office invents easy to use computer retrieval service designed to work with modified home TV
1972	BBC broadcasts experimental teletext pages in vertical blanking interval of TV signal
1973	French begin development of Antiope service
1976	BBC begins public broadcasting of CEEFAX service on two channels
1977	Experimental Antiope transmissions begin in France
1978	Canadian Department of Communications announces Telidon after eight years of research, authorizes $9.6 million for its development
1979	British Telecom division of British Post Office offers Prestel to public
1979	CAPTAIN experiment begins in Tokyo, Japan
1980	Knight-Ridder and AT&T begin viewdata test in Coral Gables, Florida
1980	German Post Office inaugurates videotext trial in Berlin and Dusseldorf
1981	AT&T publishes Presentation Level Protocol, one of seven complete technical standards required for videotext service; announces joint trial with CBS for following year
1981	French PTT begins test of Teletel viewdata service in 2500 locations in Velizy
1981	Bell Canada inaugurates trial in Toronto and Hull
1981	U.S. Federal Communications Commission authorizes broadcasters to offer commercial teletext service using any technical system they wish, declining to promulgate industry-wide standard
1981	British Telecom cuts Prestel staff and eliminates 14 regional computer centers in response to lagging demand
1982	Time Inc., Cox Cable, Times Mirror and others launch trial services in U.S.

WHAT VIDEOTEXT CAN DO

It is undeniable that videotext has many advantages over print, among them speed, selectivity, personalization of information and the maintaining of wide-ranging, comprehensive collections of data. Speed is the most striking. From the time a page of information has been written and edited until it is received by the reader takes many hours for a daily newspaper; for magazines it takes days or weeks; for books, it takes months. Little of this time is involved in the intellectual work of publishing; most is given over to setting words into type, printing and binding the publication, and then physically distributing it. This final step, the physical distribution process, often consumes as much time and cost as all the other steps together. It is carried on by a network of transport and distribution entities ranging from trucking companies, the postal service and magazine wholesalers to the corner newsstand, the retail bookstore, and the boy on his bicycle delivering the evening paper.

In a videotext system all this is short-circuited. From the moment an item is ready until it reaches the reader takes seconds, or a fraction of a second. There is no network of intermediaries: a computer takes the place of the typesetter and printer; telephone lines or the airwaves replace the trucker, the mailman and the newspaper delivery boy. The timing of the information transfer is up to the recipient of the information, not to the publisher and distributor.

The other attributes of videotext, its selectivity and ability to personalize information, also arise out of its use of computer technology. A conventional newspaper, magazine or book contains thousands of words of text, sometimes covering many different topics. No reader can be interested in every topic or every word, but the economics of producing printed publications dictate that they are printed and assembled in one physical unit, although they may be divided into sections or chapters to enable readers to quickly find what they want. In a videotext system, no reader need receive any more information than he wants; he can look at just those pages or words that are of interest, and pass over anything else. Moreover, if his interest goes beyond what he is looking at in the first instance, and if more information on that topic is part of the service, he can immediately obtain it, again by pushing the right buttons, whereas with print he would have to buy or borrow additional publications.

A computer-based videotext system can personalize information even beyond this individual selection. One way would be to maintain a list of topics in which a reader is interested and automatically alert him to new information about his subject. Another way would be to permit the user to store his own information in the system. An investor could store records on securities he owns and the prices paid—thus, punching one button would give him his own portfolio; another button current stock prices; a third button the latest brokerage recommendations. In the same way a company might store information on its export sales, to complement figures from a videotext service on foreign trade, currency and interest rates. In order not to tie up valuable storage space in the central computer, specific records of this sort would likely be kept in a personal computer or intelligent terminal, and that same piece of equipment would then be used to communicate with the computer containing videotext pages.

Personalization through a videotext service can go beyond even this feature. A user could send an inquiry directly to a publisher or information provider offering a certain type of information; the publisher would collect these inquiries regularly from the computer, and send responses either by electronic or conventional means (letter or phone). In the same way, a user could send messages to other users with similar interests.

The last advantage of videotext services, that of maintaining comprehensive yet accessible files, is less talked about, but if anything more important. For anyone who uses information a lot, the keeping of orderly, accessible files, or well-organized libraries, is a devilish problem. Physical publications come in all sizes and frequencies; they take up a great deal of space; and the specific item one is interested in often occupies a single line in a several hundred page publication. Books, newspapers and magazines have a way of being missing exactly at the moment you require them; even if the issue you want is at hand, it's not uncommon to find an article or page torn out. Even more frustrating than not being able to locate anything on a particular subject is knowing precisely the item you are seeking but not being able to put your hands on it.

In the ideal videotext system—and the word "ideal" cannot be overemphasized, since no such system exists today—the problem of maintaining files becomes far less onerous. Information does not disappear from the computer because someone else has borrowed it; it does not get frayed or torn with use; and there is no danger of a spouse or child throwing it out with the garbage.

These are some of the advantages of videotext as an information transfer medium, and they are compelling. But videotext also has significant disadvantages compared to print publications, disadvantages that have been given far too little attention in discussion of this new phenomenon. Three will be mentioned here: technical, editorial and economic.

DISADVANTAGES OF VIDEOTEXT

The technical disadvantage lies in the physical limitations of a video display terminal or TV screen for conveying information. One such limitation is that the screen holds far fewer words than a conventional printed page (even a 4 x 7-inch paperback page holds about 400 words, about three times the capacity of most videotext displays). Another is that a screen can display only one page at a time, whereas a magazine, book or newspaper permits us to look at two simultaneously. Finally, the screen isn't portable, since it must be connected to a power source and in many cases to a phone line as opposed to the newspaper or book, which can be taken to the bathroom, on the train, to the park and back and forth from the office. With all these limitations, plus the inability to vary paper, type and layout as in print, it is no wonder that video display terminals are tiresome to use for long periods, and much less flexible than print.

The editorial disadvantage of videotext is that the publisher has much less control over how the information is received than with print. A print publisher uses the order of pages, the layout, the selection of type, the size of headlines to convey his opinion of what is most important. In a videotext system, however, all information carries equal weight. If an electronic newspaper is available via videotext, nothing obligates or even encourages the reader to look at the front page headlines before turning to other sections. Also, since a videotext system usually offers information from many different publishers, no one publisher can achieve much loyalty on the part of the reader: a display of text from the editors of *Time* magazine will look physically much the same as a menu from the local restaurant. Thus, the converse of the reader's ability to select whatever he wants is the publisher's inability to organize the information as he might wish.

Although it may appear that this is a problem for publishers and not for readers, the fact is that readers depend on publishers to decide what is important and how it should be presented. The more sophisticated and knowledgeable the readers in a given field, the more able they may be to pick and choose information from a multitude of sources, and to assemble their own publications. But it's by no means a foregone conclusion that most readers either want, or will be able, to do so.

Another editorial problem rests with the completeness of information presented through videotext. Until videotext services are in wide use, there is no incentive for an information provider such as a newspaper, for example, to program in "back issues" which may contain information of interest to a user. This problem is frequently encountered when a new medium is introduced, requiring the user to search more than one source to find information. Some records may be on microform, for example, and others on paper; bibliographic online services may index only the last several years of a publication, forcing the reader to use additional, manual indexes to locate earlier citations.

The economic limitation of videotext is easy to state. In their present form such services are considerably more expensive than print publications. It can be from five or 10 to 50 times more costly to read pages over a TV screen than to read them on the printed page. And this cost does not include the cost of buying or renting the terminal, a capital expenditure that is not required when you buy a book or magazine.

DEVELOPMENT OF VIDEOTEXT SERVICES

It is too early to know how the combination of videotext advantages and disadvantages will shape the services eventually offered to consumers. There are three parties who must eventually determine whether such services succeed, and in what form. One party consists of the organizations making videotext equipment—terminals, adaptors, computers—and transmitting the signals—broadcasters, telephone companies, government-owned postal and telecommunications authorities. A second party consists of those supplying the information to go on such systems—print publishers, broadcasters, advertisers and public agencies. And the third party consists of customers for the service—businesses, professionals, educational and not-for-profit institutions, and the public at large.

To put things this way is, of course, to gloss over the complications. The three parties do not have common interests, and within each group are organizations with widely divergent—and sometimes strongly opposing—viewpoints. Thus, computer companies that make videotext terminals are quite different in outlook and business practices from the telephone companies or PTTs that will transmit the information, and both in turn are different from the broadcasters who will air teletext services. Computer companies like Digital Equipment Corp. or IBM operate in an unregulated industry characterized by a high degree of technological change: research and development budgets are a high percentage of sales, products have a short life (and consequently development costs are quickly written off), customers are predominantly companies used to investing to save money or improve efficiency. Telephone companies, by contrast, operate in a heavily regulated environment. They are not known as risk takers, do a modest amount of R&D relative to their size and have equipment installed for very long periods of time—and, consequently, depreciate their investments very slowly. Putting together companies this different to develop and market completely new information services is no easy task.

Publishers and other information providers exhibit a similar variety of characteristics. They range from giant companies like Time Inc. in the U.S. and VNU in Holland, which publish mass circulation magazines and newspapers, to highly specialized companies like Fintel in the U.K. or

Official Airline Guides in the U.S., which offer information tailored to a specific group of business customers. A publisher's attitude toward the nature and shape of a videotext service will depend directly on the type of information it offers. Figure 1.2 shows a videotext frame of information.

Finally, customers for videotext span a range every bit as broad as that of the manufacturers or information providers. Many customers will want only general information from such a service—news summaries, weather reports, sports results, perhaps shopping tips. They will be willing to pay only the most modest fee for it—perhaps $5 or $10 a month—or no fee at all. A few customers will be willing to spend substantial amounts—perhaps several hundred dollars a month—for information that is essential to their business. In between are customers who will occasionally be willing to lay out large sums for items of information that become essential at that time. Of course, the type of information required is as varied as the type available through printed publications. Statistics on the U.S. newspaper, periodical and book publishing industries demonstrate this breadth. There are 1700 daily newspapers in the U.S., and thousands more that come out less frequently. There are 1200 consumer magazines and 2700 trade magazines. There are 3900 scholarly and literary journals. More than 40,000 books are published every year.

The mechanisms for distributing these publications include newsstands, delivery boys, bookstores, wholesalers, direct mail programs, book clubs and other organizations.

All these publications and their sales channels form part of the structure of the print communications world, a structure that has been built up piece by piece over decades and centuries. For all its deficiencies, the structure ultimately serves the needs of readers, by providing information they want at a cost they are willing to pay.

No comparable structure exists for the dissemination of textual information in electronic form. Some of the building blocks for such an edifice are at hand: telecommunications circuits, decoders, editing terminals, computerized files of information. But the framework has yet to take shape. Until it does, those who presume to foretell the future of videotext in full detail, and with precise numbers on how much money will be spent in what year by how many customers, are likely to be false prophets. Erecting a structure for the dissemination of electronic information is a complicated, time-consuming, laborious undertaking to be accomplished over many years, not in the twinkling of an eye. It requires the right technology, the right economic foundation and the right habits on the part of both publishers and information users. All these must be developed by trial and error, rather than according to a master plan.

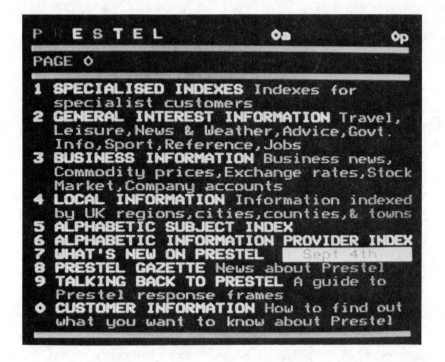

Figure 1.2 The Prestel videotext system (see Chapter 5) provides viewers with index pages that allow them to choose from among many topics for further information. Courtesy Prestel.

STATUS OF VIDEOTEXT IN 1982

The uncertain course of videotext in the future has not deterred experimentation with it. All the major industrialized countries had large-scale trials or commercial services underway by mid-1982, and it seems safe to guess that investment in this technology already runs into the hundreds of millions of dollars. Table 1.1 lists the major countries where videotext services are underway, including the type of transmission and the number of homes or terminals involved. Succeeding chapters of this book will not only describe the principal efforts underway around the world, but will also suggest what sorts of applications do and do not make sense for the future of videotext.

Table 1.1: Videotext and Teletext Services Around the World

Country	Service Name	Start Date	Transmission Medium	Number of Terminals
NORTH AMERICA				
United States	BISON (Belo Information Systems Online Network), Dallas, TX*	July 1981	telephone	190
	CBS/AT&T Videotex, Ridgewood, NJ	Fall 1982	telephone	200
	CompuServe (H&R Block), Columbus, OH	July 1980	telephone	28,000
	ConTelevision (Continental Telephone), Manassas, VA	Fall 1982	telephone	100[1] 500[2]
	Cox Cable INDAX[3] San Diego Omaha New Orleans	1981 1981 April 1982	cable cable cable	100[4] NA NA
	Dow Jones News/Retrieval	1973	telephone/cable	47,000
	FirstHand (First Bank Systems, Minneapolis), North Dakota Test	December 1981	telephone	250
	KPIX Teletext San Francisco, CA	June 1982	broadcast	100[4]
	Los Angeles Teletext Trial (KCET, KNBC, KNXT)	April 1981	broadcast	100[4]

Table 1.1: Videotext and Teletext Services (continued)

Country	Service Name	Start Date	Transmission Medium	Number of Terminals
United States (cont'd.)	The Source (Reader's Digest)	June 1979	telephone	14,100[5]
	Time Inc. Video Information Service (teletext)	October 1982	cable/satellite	400[4]
	Times Mirror Videotex, Palos Verdes and Mission Viejo, CA	March 1982	telephone/cable	350
	ViewTimes (*Danbury News-Times*), Danbury, CT (teletext)	Summer 1982	cable	50[4]
	Viewtron (Knight-Ridder/AT&T), Coral Gables, FL	July 1983	telephone	5,000
	WETA Teletext, Washington, DC	June 1981	broadcast	50
	WFLD Keyfax Teletext, Chicago, IL	April 1981	broadcast	100
	WGBH Teletext, Boston, MA	Summer 1982	broadcast	20[2]
	WKRC Teletext, Cincinnati, OH	March 1982	broadcast	40
Canada	Canatel (Canadian Government)	April 1981	packet switched network	40; 100[4]
	Grass Roots, Manitoba	1981	telephone/fiber optics	380[6]
	Mercury, New Brunswick	1980/81	telephone	45

Table 1.1: Videotext and Teletext Services (continued)

Country	Service Name	Start Date	Transmission Medium	Number of Terminals
Canada (cont'd.)	Novatex (Teleglobe Canada International)	NA	satellite/datapac	50
	Teleguide, Ontario	July 1982	dedicated telephone lines	1,200[4]
	Telidon (Alberta Government Telephone)			
	Calgary Library Trial	September 1981[7]	telephone	7
	Alberta Educational Trial	January 1982[7]	telephone	6
	Saskatchewan Telephone	September 1982	telephone	NA
	Vista (Bell Canada)	1981	telephone	490
EUROPE				
Finland	Telset	1980	telephone	310
France	Teletel (Velizy only)	mid-1981	telephone	3,000
	Electronic Directory	1981	telephone	2,000
	Private business projects	NA	NA	500
Germany	Bildschirmtext	June 1980	telephone/circuit switched network	7,700

Table 1.1: Videotext and Teletext Services (continued)

Country	Service Name	Start Date	Transmission Medium	Number of Terminals
Hungary	Teletext Test Transmission	1980	broadcast	NA
Italy	Videotel	1st quarter 1982	telephone	1,000
Netherlands	Viditel	August 1980	telephone	5,000
Norway	Teledata	1980	NA	100
Spain	Spanish Videotext Project	1978	telephone	200
Sweden	Text-TV (teletext)	1979/1980	broadcast	100,000[8]
	Teledata (videotext trial)	1979	telephone	100[9]
Switzerland	NA	November 1979	telephone	113
United Kingdom	Prestel	October 1979	telephone	16,000
	Teletext	1975	broadcast	375,000
FAR EAST				
Hong Kong	Viewdata	Spring 1982	NA	500[4]
Japan	Captain	December 1979	telephone	2,000
AFRICA				
South Africa	Beltel	1982	telephone	300

Table 1.1: Videotext and Teletext Services (continued)

Country	Service Name	Start Date	Transmission Medium	Number of Terminals
SOUTH AMERICA				
Brazil	NA	1981	NA	2,000
Venezuela	NA	1981	NA	30

*Service suspended May 1982.

NA Not available.

[1]Projected for first six months.

[2]Projected for second six months.

[3]In May 1982, Cox Cable announced a joint venture with ABC Video Enterprises to evaluate and expand existing services.

[4]Projected.

[5]As of January 1982.

[6]30 terminals incorporated from the original Ida trial; 150 are Elie terminals (fiber optic technology).

[7]Ending June 1982.

[8]As of February 1982.

[9]As of summer 1981.

Source: Compiled by Knowledge Industry Publications, Inc., based on information supplied by system owners, as well as estimates from Arlen Communications Inc.; Communications Studies and Planning International Inc.; *Guide to Electronic Publishing: Opportunities in Online and Viewdata Services*, by Fran Spigai and Peter Sommer (White Plains, NY: Knowledge Industry Publications, Inc., 1982); *The Print Publisher in an Electronic World* (White Plains, NY: Knowledge Industry Publications, Inc., 1981) and *Videotex '81* (England: Online Conferences Ltd., 1981).

2

The Technology of Videotext

by Efrem Sigel

The technology of videotext involves three separate disciplines: television broadcasting and display; computer storage and retrieval; and telephone transmission. Out of the combination of these systems has come a panoply of ways to distribute text and graphics to a video terminal. The video terminal can be a television set with special adaptor; it can be a TV monitor without the ability to receive normal broadcast programs; or it can be a screen without any ability to handle images in the normal TV standard.

TELETEXT TRANSMISSION AND DISPLAY

Teletext is the broadcast version of videotext. In this system, editors create pages or frames of information using special editing and display terminals connected to a computer (see Figure 2.1). The information is in digital form, much like the text that newspaper editors create and revise daily, using special terminals built for this purpose. In the case of teletext pages, however, the design is made to fit a standard television screen. Once the pages are finished, they are ready to be inserted into the TV broadcast signal that goes out over the airwaves. This is accomplished using a portion of the TV picture known as the vertical blanking interval (VBI). Television frames in North America and Japan consist of 525 lines of information, divided into two fields of 262½ lines each. In Europe, the standard frame is 625 lines, divided into two fields of 312½ each. (Actually, two different TV standards are in use in Europe—the French SECAM system, and the German PAL standard. Although they are incompatible they both have 625 lines.) In both the European and American systems, a certain number of lines carry no picture information; they appear as black bars at the top

Figure 2.1: Creation, Transmission and Reception of Teletext Pages

1. Editor creates teletext copy on terminal; uses special keys to indicate color for different characters, or to insert graphics.

2. Frame is reviewed, checked, then entered in computer and numbered.

3. Teletext page is multiplexed onto TV waveform signal at precise point of vertical blanking interval (VBI) lines.

4. Teletext data travels with TV signal at speed of electromagnetic waves (speed of light) to all receivers within range of TV transmitter.

5. Viewer switches teletext adaptor to "on," eliminating regular TV program and instructing adaptor to pick up and display data transmission.

6. Viewer selects number of teletext page he wishes to see.

7. When page corresponding to this number is transmitted, it is grabbed by decoder and displayed on TV screen.

or bottom of the picture on sets that are poorly adjusted.

In a teletext transmission, the frames stored as digital data are inserted or multiplexed onto the TV signal waveform in such a way that they are located in just that portion of the picture that would otherwise be blank. If the viewer at home has the proper decoding equipment, these digital signals are captured and then activate a character generator that reproduces each "page" exactly as the editor created it, and the computer stored it.

The genius of teletext, and its overriding limitation, is that pages must be continuously rebroadcast as each new TV field goes out from the transmitter. If two lines per TV field are available for a teletext page, and if all the data required to send a complete frame can be transmitted in a quarter of a second, then four teletext pages can be broadcast every second. A typical teletext magazine contains 100 pages; thus if the viewer wants to capture page 52, he will have to wait 13 seconds (on the average) until the data describing that page have been recycled for transmission to his home.

The actual timing of teletext transmission depends on the speed at which the data are transmitted; this is known as the bit per second (bps) rate. If, as in the French and British teletext systems, a teletext page contains 24 lines of 40 characters each, and if seven bits are needed to describe one character, it takes a minimum of 6720 bits to complete a page.

The technical shape of a teletext service will depend on the amount of information per page (lines per page, characters per line), i.e.:

- the number of lines in the TV frame set aside for teletext;

- the number of pages in the magazine; and

- the transmission speed (bps).

By using eight lines in the VBI instead of two, the operators of the service would have the choice of: 1) quadrupling the number of pages, while keeping access time constant; 2) keeping the number of pages constant and reducing access time by a factor of four; or 3) doubling the number of pages while halving access time.

The most dramatic increases in capacity result from full-channel teletext, which means that the entire bandwidth of a color TV channel is set aside for data transmission, with no video picture. A service of this type could easily handle 2500 to 4000 pages of teletext information, with no more waiting time for any single page than is found in the BBC's CEEFAX service at present.

Teletext Decoder

A TV set will only display teletext pages if it has the microprocessor circuitry capable of receiving digital data and converting it into a screen of text, numbers and diagrams. (See Figure 2.2.) This circuitry is contained in a device known as the decoder. The decoder is built into most teletext-equipped sets being made in Britain today; the decoders feed the data impulses into the internal circuitry of the TV set. A hand-held control, which resembles a pocket calculator (see Figure 2.3), is used to select the page the viewer wants to see: that page, once punched up, activates electronic impulses in the microprocessor to display the particular stream of data that go with the page number in question. It is only when the data desired leave the transmitter and are received at home that the page comes into view.

Designing this microprocessor circuitry is a costly, complex job of electrical engineering. The high costs associated with design, development and the capital expense of setting up a production line dictate that decoders will remain relatively expensive until mass produced. The calculator and the digital watch are perfect examples of this economic relationship. Whereas hand-held calculators cost $100 or more in the early 1970s, by the latter part of the decade they could be bought for a little as $10 or $15. In Britain today, a color TV set with a built-in teletext decoder sells for $200 or $250 more than a standard color set. Yet spokesmen for TV manufacturing companies have stated that if produced in truly large

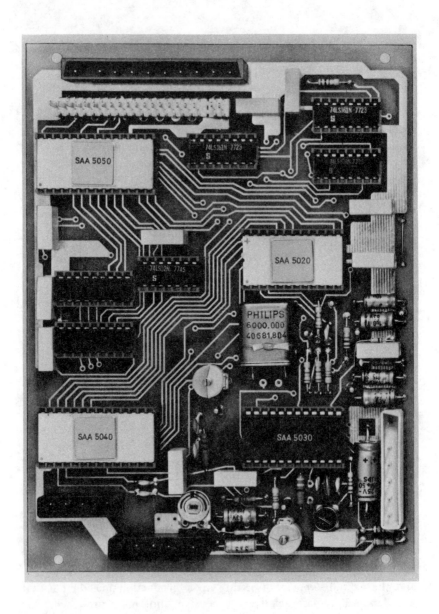

Figure 2.2 The Mullard Teletext/Viewdata decoder measures approximately 7x4½x½ inches. It contains the circuitry needed to convert digital data into material suitable for a screen display. Courtesy Mullard Limited.

quantities (hundreds of thousands, or millions), the decoder chips could drop in price so sharply that the consumer would wind up paying only an extra $50, or perhaps even as little as $20. (By the end of 1981, Mullard Ltd. had manufactured and supplied 1.2 million chip sets in six languages—European English, U.S. English, French, German, Swedish/Finnish and Italian. By the end of the following year, the figure is expected to be 2.4 million.)

Different Teletext Standards

A teletext standard has several different meanings. First, the way digital data are coded for multiplexing onto the TV waveform signal must match the way they are decoded at the receiving television set. This requires standards of transmission and display. Second, the transmission and display standards must be compatible with the broadcast system in use by a country's television stations. Since there are three principal TV transmission systems—NTSC (National Television System Committee), PAL (Phase Alternate Line) and SECAM (Sequential Couleur à Mèmoire)—compatibility among these systems is not easy to achieve.

Serial Attribute (CEEFAX) vs. Parallel Attribute (Antiope)

Several different coding schemes are possible for representing shapes by digital impulses. One scheme, used by the British Broadcasting Corporation (BBC) and the Independent Broadcasting Authority (IBA), is known as the serial attribute system. It makes use of a fixed format in which "every address in the page display store corresponds to a given character site within the page, and every stored code is either a display character or a control character," according to a BBC engineering document. This system provides for very economical use of memory—only one kilobyte of memory is required to store an entire CEEFAX page. (Slightly greater storage is required for Prestel terminals.)

Another scheme, adopted by the French for their Antiope service, is the parallel attribute method. It provides for more flexibility in data representation and transmission, but requires greater memory—approximately one kilobyte per page—and decoding of the incoming signal is slightly more complex, notes Harry E. Smith, vice president of technology at CBS Inc. Cost comparisons to date have been based on different construction techniques (off-the-shelf vs. custom large scale integrated (LSI) circuits). Smith notes that once the North American Broadcast Teletext Standard (NABTS) is integrated in LSIs, the cost differences will be marginal. Proponents of the Antiope technology, such as the CBS engineering

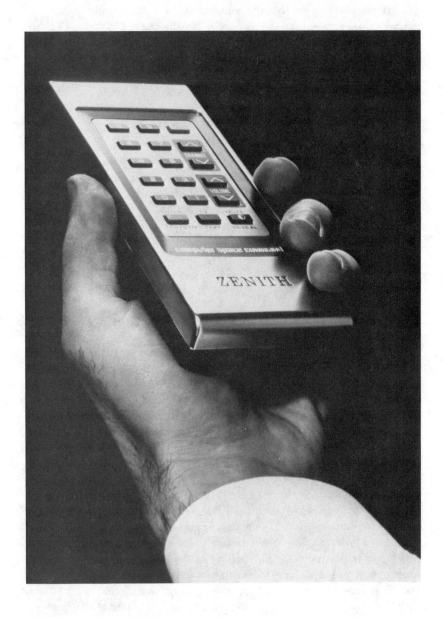

Figure 2.3 A hand held control unit is used by the viewer to select the pages of information that will appear on the viewdata screen. Courtesy Prestel.

department, have argued that the added cost in making Antiope decoders will be insignificant in mass production quantities. (CBS' NABTS filing to the Federal Communications Commission (FCC) incorporates features from Antiope, AT&T's Presentation Level Protocol and the Canadian Telidon.)

The last four years have witnessed an ongoing debate between proponents of the British and French systems in their competition to have their respective technologies adopted in other countries. As of the end of 1981 the British had a distinct lead, as teletext systems based on the BBC's CEEFAX service were operating in Holland, Germany, Belgium, Austria, Hong Kong, Finland and elsewhere. Antiope systems had been widely tested in the U.S., as well as in Spain, Italy and Australia, but had not been formally adopted anywhere.

Mosaics vs. Geometrics (Telidon)

Both Antiope and CEEFAX, and their related viewdata versions, Teletel and Prestel, employ a method of displaying graphics shapes known as mosaics. Each position on the display screen consists of a grid of six squares, two across and three down, and the filling in of varying squares with light and dark shades. This process yields a rough approximation of simple shapes. (See Figure 2.4.)

The graphics capability of Prestel, CEEFAX and Teletel/Antiope decoders can be improved by incorporating a technique known as Dynamically Redefinable Character Sets (DRCS). (See Figure 2.5.) This technique frees terminals from the restricted display of characters and graphics, by permitting new shapes and letters to be sent to the terminal from a computer or broadcast transmitter. A common videotext standard announced by the European Conference of Post and Telecommunications authorities (CEPT) in May 1981 provides for the incorporation of this technique into a new generation of terminals that could receive both Prestel and Teletel signals.

A major improvement on the mosaic method of displaying graphics comes from the Canadian videotext and teletext system, Telidon. It employs a so-called geometric display scheme, in which a microprocessor located within the terminal "draws" the desired shape after the beginning and end points of the graphic have been transmitted. This is accomplished by means of picture description instructions (PDIs) sent from the broadcast transmitter or computer center. (Figure 2.6 shows the resulting graphics on a Telidon terminal, compared to the effect achieved with a mosaic approach.)

Naturally, this improved display is more costly, since it requires greater memory and intelligence in the decoding terminal. A Telidon terminal

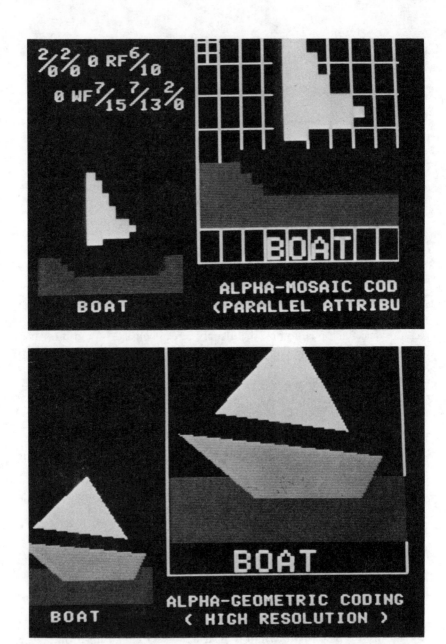

Figure 2.4 The graphic display system known as alphamosaics (top) yields shapes that are crude when compared to the alphageometric system (bottom) which provides a more refined and accurate display. Courtesy Videotex Industry Association.

employing the requisite "bit plane memory" needs 32 kilobytes of storage, vs. three kilobytes for a simple Prestel or Teletel terminal using mosaics, and six kilobytes for such a terminal using the DRCS improvement.

The Canadian Department of Communications, in a filing with the U.S. FCC, estimated that this added memory would cost about $42 (Canadian) more in 1981 prices than memory for a simple Teletel or Prestel terminal. It also estimated that by 1986 the differential would have narrowed to $14 (Canadian), as a result of continuing declines in production costs for storage chips. A Telidon terminal featuring very high resolution, and requiring 142 kilobytes of storage, was estimated to cost $200 more than the simpler competing terminals in 1981, dropping to $66 more in 1986.

The Canadian Telidon system has become a potent rival for adoption as a teletext standard, particularly since AT&T adopted a videotext display standard closer to Telidon than to other systems. (See following section on Viewdata and North American Standards.) Most countries will adopt a display system common to both teletext and viewdata so that the same decoders can display either pages transmitted by broadcasters, or pages retrieved from a computer via telephone lines. The next section will discuss viewdata technology.

VIEWDATA OR VIDEOTEXT DISPLAY

Viewdata, also known as videotext or videotex, is a computer-based information service that is actually closer to online data base distribution than to teletext. In viewdata, information is stored in a computer as entire pages; a page is called up on the subscriber's terminal by punching in the number for the page in question. Among the distinguishing features of viewdata technology are:

- very large storage capacity—limited only by what can be online in the form of computer storage discs—running into the hundreds of thousands of frames; Prestel, the world's largest viewdata service, counted 193,494 frames in use as of September 1981;

- interactive, meaning the user can specify exactly which page he wants to see, and when; and

- delivered by telephone lines or other two-way communications which link the subscriber terminal to the viewdata computer. Services in the U.K., Germany, Holland, Japan, Canada and the U.S. have all used telephone lines, but various American experiments are considering cable TV or microwave transmission.

Figure 2.5: The mosaic graphic system can be improved through the use of Dynamically Redefinable Character Sets (DRCS), a technique which allows for more flexibility in shapes and letters. Photo: Robert D. Rathbun.

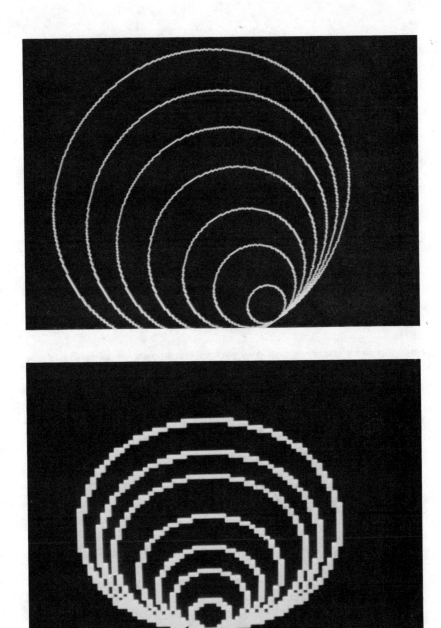

Figure 2.6 Circular lines clearly illustrate the vast improvement of the alphageometric system of graphics (top) over the alphamosaic system (bottom). Courtesy Videotex Industry Association.

The coding of information for viewdata, and the creation of pages at an editing terminal, take place in much the same way as with a teletext system. (See Figure 2.7.) The difference is that once information is in the viewdata computer it is not automatically transmitted, but remains there until called up by a subscriber. Indexing in a viewdata system can be by frame, meaning that there is no way to find a specific word, phrase or number located on a frame and to have it displayed, or it can use a keyword facility.

Figure 2.7: Creation, Transmission and Reception of Viewdata Pages

1. Editor creates viewdata page on terminal, using special keys to indicate color or graphics desired.

2. Editor assigns page number and indicates routing to and from other pages, as well as from master index.

3. Page is stored in viewdata computer, available for retrieval.

4. User switches on viewdata set, pushes button to dial viewdata computer.

5. Computer sends message to terminal to which viewer is connected and that user can begin using service.

6. User pushes button for general index, telling him categories of information available.

7. After several more detailed indexes, user is given choice of seeing page created by editor in step 1.

8. User pushes button and page is transmitted from computer along telephone lines to user's viewdata terminal.

The terminal required for a viewdata service is more complex than for teletext, mainly because of the need for two-way communications. This involves the use of a modem—a device that converts digital (computer) data into analog form for transmission over telephone lines, and then back into digital form for entry into the computer or terminal. Because a modem must either be built into a TV set, or into the adaptor attached to the set, the cost of a viewdata terminal will be comparable to that of a so-called "dumb" computer terminal, i.e., one that can enter or retrieve data, but not do any calculations or rearranging of information. Besides the modem, the main components of a viewdata terminal used in the U.K. are the microprocessor for interpreting data and displaying them as text, and the cathode ray tube (CRT) or video display screen (which can be that of an ordinary TV set). In the U.K. a viewdata set costs about £500 more than an ordinary color TV set; a viewdata adaptor which plugs into a TV set sells for about £200, or $400. In the U.S., Radio Shack sells its Videotex Color Terminal (capable of a much cruder display than Prestel, and with much less text on the screen) for $399. AT&T has stated publicly that it foresees a retail price of between $400 and $700 for a viewdata terminal capable of full color as well as far superior graphics to those available on Prestel in the U.K.

Different Viewdata/Videotext Standards

The battle over technical standards is every bit as fierce for viewdata services as for teletext. The U.K.* and France each have common standards for their viewdata and teletext services, meaning that the same sets can receive both. However, the same sets cannot receive both U.K. and French teletext or viewdata. The CEPT agreement referred to earlier would make possible terminals capable of displaying both versions, though it is impossible to know if and when this will actually take effect.

North American Standards and AT&T

The standards issue is less clearly defined in North America than in Europe. All the major European countries have government-owned postal and telecommunications authorities which enjoy a legal monopoly over telephone and telegraph traffic. Thus, if the French Direction Générale des Télécommunications (DGT) adopts its Antiope-Didon system, and if British Telecom in the U.K. adopts Prestel, the question is settled. In the U.S., however, telephone companies are privately owned and subject to government regulation, and the nature of that regulation is undergoing a complete transformation. AT&T, which accounts for 80% of telephone communications in the U.S., can set de facto standards but has no legal authority to do so. In Canada the situation is even more decentralized. Bell Canada, the largest telephone company, operates in Quebec and Ontario, whereas all the other provinces have their own phone companies, some privately owned, some owned by the provincial governments.

In North America, a viewdata standard is more a question of economics than of legal sanction. Anyone can set up a viewdata service on his own computer, connect it to the public telephone network via a value-added network like Tymnet, and sign up customers to use the service. Three or

---

*As of April 1, 1982 there were 774,385 British standard viewdata and teletext sets in operation in 15 countries. This constituted 98% of all the sets in the world.

three dozen incompatible services might result. Since AT&T has stated unequivocally that it expects a videotext business to develop and that it wants to participate in such a business, there will be great impetus to agree on transmission and display standards set forth by Bell. Otherwise, companies risk developing a market at great expense and seeing it swept away when AT&T begins offering its own videotext terminals at a much lower cost.

The Presentation Level Protocol standard set forth by AT&T on May 1, 1981 incorporated:

- both seven-bit and eight-bit coding;

- use of dynamically redefinable character sets (DRCS);

- provision for a wide range of colors through color mapping;

- provision for continuous scaling of text size;

- provision for macro-picture description instructions (PDIs); and

- ability to create images, such as signatures and logos, and to do simple animation.

(Although the standard went beyond the Canadian Telidon system in certain respects, it was much closer to what the Canadians had developed than to anything else, and Canadian firms quickly announced plans to modify their equipment to be compatible.)

Evolving Technology in Teletext and Viewdata

Existing commercial services like CEEFAX and Prestel in the U.K. use an early version of videotext technology. Already significant improvements are possible, with further enhancements under study in labs and research centers. The BBC, already operating the world's most extensive teletext service, has continued its technical research into enhancements of the system. J.P. Chambers, an engineer in the research department of the engineering division, described some of these in a June 1980 paper. At the simplest level are decoders that can store more than a page at a time; these permit the user to preprogram a sequence of pages he wishes to capture by entering the page numbers in advance. Or, if he doesn't know the page numbers, another possibility is to "link" pages of news stories to an index page so the backup frames are automatically captured by the decoder; the viewer simply presses a single digit to call these up from storage.

A further refinement of the British teletext system would be to use eight-bit codes to describe characters, instead of the seven-bit coding now in effect. This would increase the size of the alphabet in use from the present 96 characters to a maximum of 224, thus accommodating most languages written in the Latin alphabet.

The most dramatic enhancement of the teletext system would be to transmit pictures, even in full color. By defining shapes in terms of picture elements, the existing mosaic graphics can be noticeably improved; color can be added to create a "painting by numbers" effect; even full red-green-blue television picture quality can be achieved. Each of these steps requires progressively more memory in the decoder: whereas a text-only teletext page needs only a kilobyte of storage, a high-quality still TV picture needs a megabyte (1000 times as much capacity) if it is to occupy the full frame. Not only will such a decoder cost much more, but the time required to transmit such a frame will also be longer. Little wonder, then, that whatever system is experimenting with still picture transmission—and CEEFAX, Prestel, Antiope and Telidon all have shown this capability—usually restricts the area of the photo to a fraction, or inset, of the full TV picture, thus sharply reducing transmission time and required storage capacity. (See Figure 2.8.)

SOME IMPLICATIONS OF VIDEOTEXT TECHNOLOGY

During the late 1970s and early 1980s, conferences and discussions of teletext and viewdata seemed preoccupied with questions of technical standards: participants held forth about the proper bit per second rate of transmission, the merits of mosaic vs. geometric graphics, and the proper amount of memory in a terminal. This mania reached its peak at a May 1981 conference in Toronto, where AT&T first announced its Presentation Level Protocol for videotext display. Engineers from CBS, from AT&T, from the Canadian Department of Communications, from the French television and telecommunications authorities and from British Telecom (BT) held forth. Each group propounded the virtues of their systems with fervor, as journalists scratched their heads and struggled to interpret the technical jargon for readers of the next day's newspaper.

How important is the technical debate? A commonsense view might be as follows: There is no reason not to select the best technical system (provided it does not cost significantly more than a less sophisticated one), but selecting the best technical system is no guarantee of acceptance by consumers. The debate over features and standards has somewhat distracted developers from the much harder job of figuring out what information to put in a videotext system, and how to get people to use it; to this extent the debate has retarded the introduction of the technology.

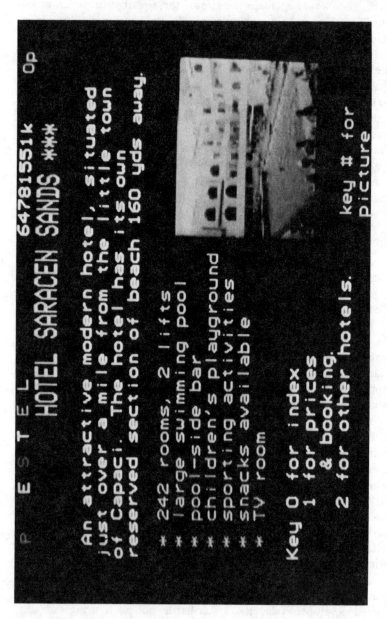

Figure 2.8 Picture Prestel offers viewers the additional feature of a photo insert along with text descriptions. Courtesy Logica Ltd.

A single-minded determination to build teletext or viewdata terminals incorporating the absolute latest in microelectronics does not, on the face of it, seem to be the right focus. New inventions have rarely been rejected because of inadequacies, provided they filled a genuine need: the first automobiles were not rejected because they had to be cranked by hand or lacked fuel-injection engines. The airplane wasn't a failure because it was originally driven by propellers, not the jet engine. Television did not suffer from being introduced though tiny black and white sets powered by vacuum tubes. All these inventions, and many more, had such overwhelming social and economic appeal that their virtues were immediately apparent, whatever the defects of the first units off the production line.

So it ought to be with videotext systems. If consumers really want to push buttons to get their TV sets to cough up information on demand, it is presumably because they appreciate the speed and convenience of this sort of information service—not because they are impressed by the engineers' ability to come close to the resolution of full color photographs in *Life* magazine or the Neiman-Marcus catalog.

All the successful computerized information retrieval services today use simple black and white displays, sometimes even with all capital letters. The absence of color, graphics and other aesthetically pleasing features may be an annoyance, but it has not hurt organizations like Dow Jones/News Retrieval, Mead Data Central with LEXIS, or Lockheed with its Dialog data base service, in selling computerized information to the business or legal and academic community. At the other extreme, it is hard to imagine any videotext display, no matter how visually captivating, that will get 20 million Americans to switch off "Monday Night Football" in order to check platinum futures or the vote totals in a British parliamentary by-election.

The argument is not that technology cannot contribute to the appeal, and eventual success of videotext. Rather, it is that preoccupation with "the best system"—an argument that has had strong political overtones because of the national rivalries involved—has obscured other, more important decisions about how to organize a videotext service that will appeal to consumers.

The next chapter will consider the nature of information sold in the business and consumer markets, and which of that information is best suited to a videotext system.

3

Videotext and the Nature of Information Services

by Efrem Sigel

If it is to be developed at all, videotext must flourish as an information service, not as a technology. Among the important questions, therefore, for those seeking to introduce videotext services are:

- what is the proper audience for these services;

- what type of information is best suited to electronic dissemination in general and videotext display in particular; and

- whether videotext can be used for transactions like shopping or banking.

VIDEOTEXT: BUSINESS OR CONSUMER MEDIUM

The first question to be considered is: what is the most logical audience for these services—business/professional, or consumer?

The business and professional market consists of companies, professional organizations (law firms, medical partnerships), universities and research centers and individual practitioners like lawyers, consultants or accountants. Information services directed to these groups are aimed at providing news of an industry or profession, or improving professional or business skills. The information is either bought directly by the business, or by an individual who can deduct it as a business expense.

In contrast, the consumer market consists of individuals who use information at home and pay for it out of their own pockets. Although the information may be related in some way to the person's occupation, he or she is acquiring it out of personal interest or the desire for self-improvement, not to meet a specific business need.

Because a videotext service can be transmitted over telephone lines to a modified TV set, it is often assumed that consumers are the principal users of such services. However, phones reach business offices as well as homes, and a computer terminal or other video display terminal will do just as well as a TV set for displaying text. The real determinant of what sort of videotext service makes sense is the information it provides in relation to the needs of the customer.

Business/Professional Information Services

Business and professional users spend upwards of $9 billion per year for published information, and many times that sum for internal information. Internal information for business takes the form of studies and memos, computerized sales and accounting and inventory reports; meetings and presentations. Though the manifestation of this information flow is a blizzard of paper, microfilm, computer tape and discs, these media account for only a fraction of the true cost of information. The largest expenditures go for the salaries of information workers: managers, secretaries and assistants, researchers, forecasters, accountants, purchasing agents and dozens of other job categories. The salaries of all white-collar workers in the U.S. total nearly $800 billion annually. In a real sense the product of all these millions of people is information—in the form of numbers, memos, reports and presentations. However, that information is not the final product of most businesses, but only a necessary ingredient in the production process.

Information *is* the final product of publishers, broadcasters, market research companies and others who sell to business, and while these total sales are only a fraction of what business spends on information, they still add up to a significant sum. A study of the business information markets estimates that revenues of business information suppliers were $8.9 billion in 1981. The study depicts the principal segments of that total as shown in Table 3.1.

One of the best indicators of the potential for videotext in the business and professional market is the amount being spent to acquire information in computerized form. According to the figures in Table 3.1, all data bases, both in printed and electronic formats, generate $2.6 billion in revenue. However, the portion that is distributed online is only a fraction of this total—estimated at $680 million in 1981.

A tabulation done by *IDP Report* newsletter shows that the market for online data bases has been growing by more than 80% per year for the last five years, although the rate of growth has slowed, since 1980, to perhaps 40% a year. Table 3.2 shows some of the principal indicators.

Table 3.1: Business Information Revenues by Segment, 1981

Segment	Revenues (in millions)
Trade magazines	2,156
Data bases	2,610
Newsletters and loose leaf services	1,018
Research services	520
General business periodicals and services	800
Trade shows and seminars	1,660
Books	155
Total	8,919

Source: *The Business Information Markets 1982-87* (White Plains, NY: Knowledge Industry Publications, Inc. 1982).

Table 3.2: Growth in Online Services

	1975	1977	1979	1981
Number of Online Data Bases	301	362	528	1,028
Number of Records[1]	33,000,000	50,000,000	116,000,000	200,000,000
Number of Customers	under 5,000	17,000[2]	57,500[2]	199,145

[1] Bibliographic data bases only.
[2] 1977 and 1979 figures interpolated on basis of 84% annual growth rate.
Source: *The Business Information Markets 1982-87* (White Plains, NY: Knowledge Industry Publications, Inc., 1982.)

Speed and convenience are the obvious reasons that online data bases have enjoyed such growing acceptance in the business world. Certainly these data bases are not cheap to use. Hourly rates for services offered by Lockheed's Dialog, Dow Jones and Mead Data Central range as high as $125 or $150 per hour; even inexpensive data bases can cost from $35 to $75 per hour. Since many data base customers spend several hundred dollars a month to use these services, they must feel that the expenditure is worth it.

Types of Business/Professional Information, and Suitability for Electronic Dissemination

Though we are accustomed to classifying information products by form or medium (magazine, book, newsletter, TV program), it may be more helpful to examine information in terms of its role in the decision-making process and other professional activities. Such a classification will also point up the suitability of different types of information for electronic dissemination.

Analyses done by the editors at Knowledge Industry Publications, Inc., suggest five categories of business and professional information:

1) *Transaction-oriented information*—names and addresses, prices, stock quotes, items for sale. Availability of this information leads directly to a transaction, such as a phone call, letter or purchase.

2) *Decision-oriented information*—facts, numbers, opinions, impressions—used directly to make a decision. Numbers gathered by independent research services, like the Nielsen television ratings, are an example of information that leads directly to a decision, e.g., take a show off the air.

3) *Background decision information*—consisting of the same sources as in (2), but not used the same way: the reader assimilates the information for use in the future, rather than immediately.

4) *General interest information*—from newspapers, trade magazines, radio, TV, conferences, personal conversations. This type of information is much more diffuse and random than in categories 1, 2 and 3, and contributes to a manager or professional's general awareness, rather than to specific decisions he must make.

5) *Skills-oriented information*—techniques of management, sales, accounting, etc. Such information usually comes from a combination of face-to-face, printed and audiovisual sources.

In general, the more information is used for a transaction or a decision, the higher the price it commands—and the more the recipient is willing to pay for the speed and convenience of electronic delivery. In addition, because information in these two categories often consists of specific facts, numbers, names, addresses, etc., it is particularly suited to display on a screen. Electronic information services are best when the user needs to retrieve specific facts, and worst when the user needs to read an entire document or browse through a mass of material. Figure 3.1 shows the different types of information, and their suitability for electronic dissemination.

**Figure 3.1: Types of Business/Professional Information
and Suitability for Electronic Dissemination**

Category of Information	Example	Suitability for Electronic Dissemination
1. Transaction-oriented	Names, addresses, stock quotes, classified ads	Good to excellent
2. Decision-oriented	Facts, numbers, survey information, financial information	Good
3. Background decision	Same as above	Good
4. General interest	Newspaper articles, sales reports, information for meetings and seminars	Poor to fair
5. Skills-oriented	How-to techniques of management, sales, accounting	Poor

The Consumer Market for Information

Although supplying information to consumers is a multi-billion dollar business for the world's broadcasters and newspaper, magazine and book publishers, no one can say for certain exactly what influences consumers to choose one medium over another, or any medium at all, to acquire information. Education, social class, occupation and personal preference all play a role; it is obvious that the people who watch a televised opera from New York City's Lincoln Center have different tastes than those who, at the same hour, choose to view "Laverne and Shirley." The person who subscribes to *Scientific American* displays distinct differences from one who picks up the *National Enquirer*. Some broad generalizations are available to distinguish heavy TV watchers from devoted magazine readers; for example, the former are depicted by researchers as less well educated and more passive, the latter as better educated and more active. But these broad statements may tell less than they seem to. TV watching, after all, is well established in every age group, social and educational class, and most adults read some publication, whether it is the daily newspaper, a favorite magazine or a bestselling book.

One helpful guide to media behavior is the attempt to understand the different functions that media perform for individuals. In a paper published by the Harvard Program on Information Resources Policy, Christine Urban identifies three such functions: 1) information acquisition, or "surveillance"—people use the media to locate specific facts, from train schedules to box scores to what the Prime Minister of Great Britain said yesterday; 2) social connection—broad information of use in social situations; and 3) escape—diversions from day to day cares through fiction, movies, TV entertainment.[1]

Although these categories are different from those shown in Figure 3.1 for business and professional information, they too can be ranked according to their suitability for electronic dissemination. Only the information in the first category is well-suited to electronic display; once again the determining characteristic is the search for specific facts that can be viewed on a screen.

Consumers' need to acquire specific facts, however, is not by itself enough to support a computer-based videotext service. The consumer market for information services has marked differences from the business and professional market, principally with regard to how information is paid for. Newspapers and magazines are the largest segment of the consumer market and these publications derive most of their revenues from advertising, rather than from reader outlays. Books are the next largest segment; when measured in terms of customer outlays rather than publishers' receipts, books significantly outrank magazines. A striking characteristic of the three major printed consumer information media— newspapers, magazines and books—is their very low cost per unit of information, per page or per word. In part this reflects advertiser support of a large part of the cost of publication; in part the fact that purchase of a magazine or book is highly discretionary.

Whereas the lawyer has no choice but to subscribe to a looseleaf service in his area of specialty, the consumer need not buy any book for recreational reading. He can go fishing, watch TV or garden in his leisure time; if he does read, he can choose from over 400,000 books in print at any one time. This choice acts to keep the price of publication down, and to force publishers to seek the widest market for any title. There are some fields of consumer information in which publishers consciously seek to produce higher priced books or magazines for a narrow audience— expensive art books, sometimes in limited editions, or encyclopedia sets— but these are the exception.

Also when it comes to consumer information services, audiovisual formats—notably radio and television—help to dampen the price that can be charged for printed publications. Services supported entirely by advertising, TV and radio, appear "free" to the consumer, once he has bought the receiver. Only since the mid-1970s have consumers begun to spend large sums out of their own pockets to receive TV programs via cable television, or to buy prerecorded programs on video cassette or disc.

Table 3.3 shows the outlays by consumers for entertainment and information services. To illustrate the difference between publisher or supplier receipts and consumer expenditures, both sets of figures are given.

Table 3.3: Consumer Information and Entertainment Services:
Consumer Outlays and Supplier Receipts, 1980
(in millions)

Category	Consumer Outlays	Supplier Receipts
Newspaper circulation	$5,100	$3,500
Book purchases	$6,670	$6,420
Motion picture admissions	$2,748	$1,760
Magazine circulation	$3,600	$2,100
Cable and pay TV subscriptions	$2,238	$2,238

Source: Knowledge Industry Publications, Inc., estimates.

Several conclusions stand out after examining this pattern of consumer spending for information services. One is the extremely modest level of outlays per household for even the largest categories of information. Consumer purchases of $5.1 billion annually on newspapers are significant, but measured against 80 million households, that sum works out to only $63.75 per year. And the newspaper is the only one of the printed consumer services that is nearly universal in its reach. Whereas 75% of all households buy a newspaper every day, the proportion that subscribe to magazines or buy books is far smaller. Surveys show that about 60% of all households subscribe to one or more magazines. The circulation of the 100 largest consumer magazines totals 228.9 million.[2] This works out to about three magazines per household. At a typical subscription price of $16 per year, consumer outlays for magazines are approximately $3.6 billion annually.

As for book purchases, a smaller proportion of consumers buy books than subscribe to newspapers or magazines. Whereas 75% of households take a daily paper, and whereas magazine circulation averages three per home, surveys show that less than half the adults in the U.S. have read a book in the past six months. The only truly large volume books in the U.S. are mass market paperbacks; about 550 million of these are sold annually. If we assume, arbitrarily, that 25% of these copies go to schools, libraries and individual students, that leaves consumer sales of 413 million, or an average of five per household. Studies have consistently found that a large share of paperback sales are made to a small minority of purchasers, some of whom buy or read a book per month.

COST PER UNIT OF INFORMATION— CONSUMER VS. BUSINESS SERVICES

Since books, with rare exceptions, carry no advertising, consumers pay the entire cost of information. This explains why even paperbacks have much stiffer cover prices than do newspapers or magazines. A revealing way of analyzing what consumers pay for printed information services, and one that is useful in comparing print and electronic delivery, is to measure that cost per page and cost per word. Table 3.4 does this for four examples of printed consumer publications: *The New York Times* (daily), *Reader's Digest* (monthly), a bestselling paperback, *The Covenant,* by James Michener, published by Fawcett Books and *Webster's New Collegiate Dictionary,* published by the G.& C. Merriam Co.

Table 3.4: Unit Cost of Information in Newspapers, Magazines and Books

	Price	Number of pages	Number of words	Cost per page	Cost per 1000 words
The New York Times	$.30	40	120,000	$.0075	$.0025
Reader's Digest	1.29	110	40,000	.0100	.0300
The Covenant	4.75	800	400,000	.0060	.0100
Webster's New Collegiate Dictionary	21.95	1,532	8,000,000	.0140	.0030
Average Cost				.0090	.0100

Source: Knowledge Industry Publications, Inc.

Table 3.5 gives a similar analysis for business information publications including *Business Week* magazine, the *Encyclopedia of Associations* published by Gale Research Co., the *Daily Report for Executives,* a newsletter from the Bureau of National Affairs and the *Federal Tax Reporter* from Commerce Clearing House. While it is misleading to compare information services purely on such quantitative criterion as the cost per physical unit of information, the magnitude of such cost does give a useful guide for understanding how consumer and business information services differ. Thus, the significance of Tables 3.4 and 3.5 can be summarized in a single, stark comparison: the business services cost 18 times more per page and 31 times more per thousand words than the consumer services. (See Table 3.6.)

Striking as this difference is, it is actually understated as a result of including *Business Week* in the business information services tabulation. *Business Week* is usually classified as a consumer magazine because of the breadth of its readership; certainly it resembles consumer magazines in its economic underpinning which relies on advertising for more than three

Table 3.5: Unit Cost of Information in Business Magazine, Directory, Newsletter and Looseleaf Service, 1981

	Price	Number of pages	Number of words	Cost per page	Cost per 1000 words
Business Week single issues	$2.00	160	50,000	$.033	$.04
one year subscription	$34.95				
Encyclopedia of Associations (annual)	$140.00	1,600	1,100,000	$.087	$.127
Daily Report for Executives one year subscription	$3,175	7,500	13,750,00	$.42	$.85
Federal Tax Guide Reports one year subscription	$230.00	1,950	1,053,000	$.12	$.22
Average of 4 publications				$.165	$.31
Average of 3 publications (excluding *Business Week*)				$.209	$.40

Source: Knowledge Industry Publications, Inc.

Table 3.6: Ratio of Unit Costs of Business to Consumer Information Services

	Per page	Per 1000 words
Average cost per page, 4 consumer publications	$.009	$.01
Average cost, 4 business publications	$.165	$.31
Average cost, 3 business publications (excluding *Business Week*)	$.209	$.40
Ratio, business to consumer (with *Business Week*)	18:1	31:1
Ratio, business to consumer (without *Business Week*)	23:1	40:1

Source: Knowledge Industry Publications, Inc.

quarters of its revenue. Without *Business Week*, the business service turns out to cost 23 times more per page and 40 times more per thousand words than the consumer publication. Although the role of advertising in certain publications is a central one, this enormous disparity in cost cannot be explained solely by the absence of advertising in many business services. Note that the paperback listed in Table 3.4, *The Covenant*, has the lowest cost per page, and the second lowest cost per word, of the three publications analyzed.

Though we haven't included audiovisual services in this analysis, it would be perfectly feasible to do so. One result would be that TV and radio are incredibly cheap to the consumer when measured on a cost per word basis. Even where consumers pay for video information, as in monthly cable TV subscription fees, the cost turns out to be infinitesimally small. A cable system with 30 channels, averaging 15 hours per channel per day, will give the consumer access to 13,500 hours of programming per month at an average cost of $9. Each hour probably contains at least 9000 words of spoken information (there's no ready way to count visual images) and the number of words transmitted comes to a staggering total of 121.5 million words a month for a cost per thousand words of $.00007. Even if we divide this by 30, in recognition that an individual can watch only one channel at a time regardless of how many choices he has, the total words transmitted is still 4.1 million for a cost per thousand words of $.0002.

IMPLICATIONS FOR VIDEOTEXT SERVICES

The point of all this discussion about the cost of existing information services is to see what we can learn about videotext. The world of existing information services is complex, sometimes confusing, often untidy. But it is a world in which customers daily hand over hundreds of millions of dollars and receive information in return. If we want to know what kind of information people want, the form in which they want it and the value that they set on it, we have no better guide than their present behavior.

It must be said that there is a temendous air of unreality about many discussions of videotext because they are not grounded in economic experience. Few such services around the world are receiving any money from customers. The largest commercial service, British Telecom's Prestel in England, is receiving money, but estimates are that Prestel is spending up to several times as much as it is receiving. Even if this ratio were to be reduced somewhat, it's not a state of affairs that can go on very long. The cuts in staff and computer centers announced by Prestel in late 1981 reflect this fact.

Looking at the cost of information in conventional printed services gives us some groundwork for examining the costs of electronic services, whether in an online computer data base or in videotext form. The main problem in making the comparison is that printed services are sold outright; cost remains the same whether the customer reads all of a publication or only a fraction; whether he glances at it briefly and throws it away—as in the case with many daily newspaper readers—or whether he keeps it on the desk or by the bedside to refer to repeatedly—as might be done with any number of publications from an industry directory, to the *Guiness Book of World Records* or the *Bible*.

Most electronic information services today charge predominantly by time—the minutes or hours that a customer is connected to the computer. Some also charge per unit of information retrieved, e.g., about 15 cents per *Chemical Abstracts* citation displayed on a VDT or printed out, or five cents for a listing of London restaurants on Prestel, courtesy of the Consumers Association. And a few have an annual subscription fee, or requirement that the customer receive a printed publication in order to use the online service.

Charging by the clock favors the online customer who knows exactly what he wants, uses the computer to get it with a minimum of wasted time, then moves on to something else. A journal citation from Engineering Index, a summary from the New York Times Information Bank, the latest gold bullion prices on Prestel, may cost him $2 or $5 or 50 cents, but that is the total expenditure. There is no hunt for the information in a book, no time-consuming trip to the library. Paying by the clock can be far more expensive than using a print publication, however, if the same publication is consulted repeatedly over time.

To compare the cost of print publications that carry a one-time price with electronic services charging by the clock, is not a straightforward exercise. It can be done, however, with the aid of a few assumptions. Let's take two examples: a printed newspaper compared to its electronic alternative, and a business directory.

Printed Newspaper vs. Electronic Newspaper

A printed newspaper like *The New York Times*, as noted in Table 3.4, contains 40 full-sized pages of editorial information, with approximately 120,000 words of text. It costs the consumer 30 cents on the newsstand, perhaps 50 cents delivered at home. The cost per 1000 words is $.0025 (less than three-tenths of a cent), or $.0041 delivered at home.

An alternative to buying the *Times* is to subscribe to The Source, one of two leading information services available online. The Source charges customers $5.75 per hour in evening hours and delivers information to a VDT or home computer attached to TV set, at a rate of 300 characters per second. The Source is capable of displaying 25 lines of 80 characters each, or 2000 characters, although many displays contain fewer characters. Assume that a Source subscriber uses the service for 12 minutes a night to scan the day's headlines and news stories from United Press International, to see sports results, to look at stock market highlights, including closing prices of selected companies. In 12 minutes the customer might look at 20 complete screens of information, containing 225 words each, or a total of 4500 words. The cost on his Source bill will be $1.15 in computer time. The cost of the telephone time, making a local call during evening hours, will be roughly 12 cents, for a total of $1.27. The comparison between the printed and electronic newspaper then looks as follows:

	The New York Times	The Source	Ratio
Total cost	$.30	$1.27	1:4.20
Cost per 1000 words	$.00025	$ .282	1:110

In other words, The Source is four and a third times more expensive than the *Times* on an absolute cost basis; it is 110 times more expensive on a cost-per-thousand words basis.

Printed vs. Online Business Directory

The comparison between a print and online version of a business directory presents a slightly different picture. As noted in Table 3.5, the print version of the *Encyclopedia of Associations* costs $140, and has 1600 pages of information with approximately 1.1 million words of text. The cost per thousand words is $.127, or about 13 cents.

The online version of the *Encyclopedia of Associations* is available from Dialog (a major information retrieval service). Dialog charges $55 per connect hour (not including telecommunications charges) to access the *Encyclopedia of Associations* data base, and can deliver information to customers with Dialog-compatible terminals at a rate of 120 characters per second.

For an online user, the cost for 10, 30 and 50 lookups per year (assuming each lookup takes three minutes) would be as follows (not including telecommunications charges of from $5 to $8 per hour):

10 lookups = $ 27.60
30 lookups = $ 82.80
50 lookups = $138.00

The cost comparison between owning the printed directory and subscribing to the online version looks as follows:

	Print directory	Dialog	Ratio
10 lookups	$140.00	$ 27.60	5.:1
30 lookups	$140.00	$ 82.80	1.7:1
50 lookups	$140.00	$138.00	1.01:1

For the occasional user (10 lookups per year), the cost of owning the print directory is about five times as expensive as subscribing to the online version; for the moderate user (30 lookups per year), it's about one and half times more expensive; and for the frequent user (50 lookups per year), the cost is about equal.

The implications of the preceding discussion can be summarized succinctly. Whereas business and professional customers are used to paying large amounts of printed information, and are increasingly ready to pay even more for the convenience of online access, residential consumers have no such disposition. Consumers pay only modest sums out of their own pockets for newspapers, magazines and books. Much of the cost of newspapers and magazines is subsidized by advertising. The fact that most such consumer purchases are discretionary causes intense competition on the part of publishers, thus keeping prices low. When measured by the quantity of information transmitted, even supposedly low-priced online services like The Source actually cost 100 times as much as the printed newspaper.

If consumers won't pay for videotext services out of their own pockets, then the consumer market is just not a good bet for videotext. However, there are several ways in which consumers might not have to pay directly for such a service.

The most obvious is broadcast teletext. In this case information will be provided free of charge by a broadcaster; in the U.K. the cost is borne by TV license fees; in the U.S. it would probably be borne by advertising. Since costs of storage and transmission are low, and since much of the information is gathered anyway by existing news staffs, there is little economic obstacle to the introduction of teletext. It need not be a service with mass appeal, but it ought to have a market.

Beyond the market for teletext, however, there are interesting possibilities for advertiser-supported information in computer-based videotext systems. There are also prospects for transaction services in which computer processing actually saves the customer money. The following section will discuss several possiblities.

Transaction Services vs. Information Services

Although consumers shell out $21 billion a year for information (see Table 3.3), this is not a large sum when held up against the total of consumer spending, or even the amount of purely recreational spending. People in the U.S. pay $5.1 billion for newspapers, but $34.2 billion for beer, wine and liquor. And the $6.7 billion for books shrivels in comparison with what is spent annually on cosmetics, $30.7 billion.

Because the retail distribution system involves such heavy costs in moving goods from one place to another, and because customers must devote so much time to finding the things they need to buy, one obvious use of electronic communication systems like videotext is simply marketing for marketers and shopping for shoppers.

In concept the idea is wonderfully appealing. The computer stores many thousands of items for sale, with descriptions, prices and names of suppliers. Information might come from a variety of sources. A huge retailer like Sears Roebuck could give customers electronic access to its catalog—thousands of individual products from a single source. Diagrams or even color photographs of certain products could be stored and transmitted at the touch of a button. After the user has looked at the description of an item, he could then decide to order it. Touching a few more keys would send his credit card or account number to the central computer, which would check his credit and flash an acknowledgement of the order. The supplier, in this case Sears, could use the computer record to produce an invoice, a confirmation or packing slip, and any other paper work to finish the transaction.

Developing such a shopping service involves many problems. But awakening a consumer desire to shop at home is not one of these. Shopping from catalogs or by mail order is already an enormous business in the U.S. One estimate places it at more than $100 billion annually. It has been growing by 11% a year, compared to the 10% rate for retail sales in general. The business is smaller overseas, but still important. In Britain mail order sales are more than $4 billion; in Germany more than $8 billion.[3]

In all these cases the sums are much larger than the outlays for printed publications. If a videotext system can really operate in the manner sketched above, as a giant catalog shopping service, it has the potential of many billions of dollars annually in transactions.

Such a service has another aspect that should be of special interest to newspaper and periodical publishers—or broadcasters—who derive most or all of their revenues from advertising. Advertising today is sold by space or time; the publisher or broadcaster gets paid regardless of how successful the ad is, but if the ad is very successful the publisher gets not a penny more than if it is modestly worthwhile. In a videotext service organized by, say a daily newspaper, this relationship between publisher and advertiser could change significantly. Nothing prevents the videotext system organizer from having an economic stake in the transactions resulting from use of the service. The stake could be a handling charge per order, or a percentage of the value of the order. In either case, the system owner stands the chance of much greater profit than in simply selling advertising space, because he performs the role of active middleman, something that is not the case with conventional one-way printed services.

If the potential in marketing is great, so are the opportunities in financial services. The number of checks processed annually in the U.S. is beginning to approach the number of grains of sand on the beach. In 1980 the figure was 39 billion.[4] At a cost per check estimated at 40 cents, the banking industry spends $15.6 billion just for the physical handling of this paper avalanche. According to several banking organizations, many thousands of people in the banking industry work on check clearing, many of them on night shifts, so that the banks can open their doors to the public every morning showing accurate balances in their accounts.

Electronic funds transfer is not a new subject in banking; it has been the subject of exhaustive study for at least a decade. But the problem of getting citizens to accept and use complex computer terminals to do their banking is a formidable obstacle. Videotext offers a way out of this dilemma. Videotext services use equipment designed to be low cost, and computer protocols that are easy to learn. They offer access to a variety of information and entertainment services. If videotext can be a way of introducing computer equipment into the home, speedy and convenient financial services could be a way of getting people to use that equipment.

This was the rationale behind the decision of Bank One in Columbus, OH, which joined with OCLC in 1980 to test videotext in that community. The bank allowed depositors to pay bills using their terminals, while the same terminals were used to access information from the data bases gathered by OCLC for the test. This is not the only test of electronic banking to take place in recent years. United American Service Corp., a bank holding company in Knoxville, TN, has placed terminals in the homes of 300 customers. BankAmerica in California and Citicorp and Chemical Bank in New York are among the giant financial institutions experimenting with electronic banking; American Express, a 50% owner of Warner Amex, a leading cable TV company, is another likely candidate for electronic banking services. A Minneapolis bank holding company, First Bank Systems Inc., in its videotext experiment known as FirstHand, has placed 250 terminals in customers' homes to test, among other things, customer willingness to do banking through a modified TV set. Electronic bill paying is part of the Teletel 3V trial in Velizy, France and will also be a feature of the CBS-AT&T test in Ridgewood, NJ.

Transactions like shopping and banking are candidates for videotext for another reason besides their sheer size in economic terms. That reason is that in one form or another these activities are obligatory. We can do without a subscription to *Time* magazine, but none of us can go without purchasing the dozens of goods and services—from food to property insurance—that are essential to daily living. In the same vein, a person need not read the paper every day, let alone subscribe to its videotext equivalent, but he can hardly dispense with writing checks or otherwise paying for what he buys. Since shopping and paying for purchases must take place anyway, if electronics makes it possible to do them more cheaply or easily, there is every incentive to adopt these new systems.

TRANSACTION COMPANIES AS INFORMATION SUPPLIERS

Companies engaged in banking, financial services, direct marketing or other transaction services are among the most sophisticated users of computerized information services in a modern society. American Express, for example, maintains computerized records on 13.3 million cardholders. Visa and MasterCard holders are believed to number more than 158 million. An estimated 39 billion checks are processed annually—which works out to about 2.7 million checks per bank. The worldwide banking industry has developed special computer and telecommunications networks like SWIFT (Society for Worldwide Interbank Financial Transfers) to speed the settlement of transactions among members around the globe. In fall 1981, U.S. banks began a system whereby credits or debits with European banks were handled the same day, instead of overnight, as previously had been the case. Electronic communication has become the cornerstone of international financial and commodity markets that never shut down—when the London Stock Exchange is finished for the day, New York is still going; when New York closes, the Pacific Exchange is still open, and so on around the globe. A telephone or telex machine and a terminal that can be plugged into any computer around the world, are all that a trader needs to be in business, whatever time it is according to the office clock on the wall.

Although not as dependent on instantaneous information, large companies engaged in direct marketing are just as sophisticated in using computerized information resources. The R.H. Donnelley division of Dun & Bradstreet, and R.L. Polk Co., maintain computerized files of upwards of 100 million names and addresses for U.S. residents. These files are the basis for a vast mailing list business, as well as for other marketing services involving economic projections, location of new stores or plants, etc. Individual marketers like Sears Roebuck or Montgomery Ward have lists of catalog customers that run into the millions as well.

For certain industries, like airline travel, the existence of a computerized information system is more essential than the existence of the industry's production facilities. An airline can keep functioning if one or two of its planes are grounded for repairs, but it can operate with only the greatest difficulty if its computerized reservation system grinds to a halt. Backup for the computer system is more important than backup for any single plane.

The information stored in these proprietary computer systems is of varying usefulness. Some of it, like a list of yesterday's airline passengers, may be virtually worthless. Other information, like the names and addresses of American Express members who spend $1000 a month with their cards, can be of enormous commercial value. Videotext technology raises the possiblity that this information can be exploited: a marketer can use a videotext system as a means of addressing messages to its best customers. A bank can use terminals installed on customers' premises to deliver other information besides the day's balance. Once a customer is linked to an information provider's terminal, for whatever purpose, the link is a highway along which other information may travel.

It is this fact of modern computer technology that threatens to change the way information is bought and sold in modern societies. If a publisher is someone who has information, an audience, and a way of getting the information to the audience, then Sears Roebuck in Chicago, Barclay's Bank in London and Nomura Securities in Tokyo fit the definition of publisher as well as *The New York Times*, the firm of William Collins & Sons, or the Japanese newspaper publisher, Nihon Keizai Shimbun.

SUMMARY

Understanding the role of videotext services requires an understanding of how customers acquire information for business or personal use. Because this process is so complex, there can be no straightforward answers concerning the market for videotext. Nevertheless, the following general conclusions can be offered:

1) the business/professional market is far more promising in the near term than is the consumer market;

2) whether the market is business or consumer, the retrieval of specific facts is the most logical videotext application; and

3) videotext services may first appear in homes as a way of conducting shopping or banking; the purchase of information for its own sake should be a more limited activity.

NOTES

1. Christine Urban, *Factors Influencing Media Consumption: A Survey of the Literature* (Cambridge, MA: Harvard University, Program on Information Resources Policy, 1981).

2. Benjamin M. Compaine, *The Business of Consumer Magazines* (White Plains, NY: Knowledge Industry Publications, Inc., 1982), p. 50.

3. Direct Mail Marketing Association, 6 E. 43 St., New York, NY 10017, 1982.

4. American Bankers Association, 1120 Connecticut Ave., NW, Washington, DC 20036, 1982.

5. Data from 1981 American Express annual report.

4

Videotext in the United States

by Jeffrey Silverstein

INTRODUCTION

Development of videotext in the United States began in 1978 and has followed two paths. The first and best developed path to date is to graft the new generation of high quality videotext displays to the existing online retrieval business. Such retrieval services primarily serve business, professional and academic customers. Consumer-oriented videotext, on the other hand, has been slower to develop.

Online information distributors like Mead Data Central, Dow Jones News/Retrieval and Dialog serve the first market. These services developed quickly by filling the specialized information needs and sometimes just the raw curiosity of wealthy institutional customers. These customers could afford both the capital costs and relatively high unit charges for electronically delivered non-graphic information. These early systems delivered information over telephone lines, which avoided problems of interference with other services and thus minimized regulatory problems.

The business and professional online services grew rapidly in 1981. Ten leading distributors of electronically delivered information averaged annual revenue growth of more than 30% during 1981, according to a tabulation made by *IDP Report*.[1] Customer growth for 20 top data base distributors was more than 26% during the same period, a growth rate far above national economic expansion. Twenty top data base distributors had nearly 200,000 customers by the beginning of 1982. All these services use simple black and white terminal displays with none of the color or sophisticated graphics possible in other technologies, e.g., Telidon, Prestel and Antiope (see Chapter 2). Their growth seems to suggest that customers, at least in the business markets, are more interested in retrieving the right facts than in watching pretty displays on the screen.

Consumer-oriented videotext has been slower to develop and more complex. This is partly because videotext rules have not been established, partly because of uncertainty over the importance of graphics to the consumer, and partly because no one knows what people will pay for information retrieval at home. The ability of personal computers to run video game programs may help fuel the growth of home information retrieval, because the popularity of games is enhancing the purchase of personal computers, which in turn boosts the market potential for information retrieval services.

Without the benefit of government sponsored research and development programs, consumer-oriented videotext in the U.S. began in 1978 as a hesitant trial using technologies developed in Europe and Canada. But once products were developed enough to demonstrate, the U.S.—with more than 80 million homes equipped with both televisions and telephones—was clearly targeted as the world's most fertile videotext soil. Foreign agencies and manufacturers rushed to show their wares, even though none had figured out how to market successfully on their home ground. Table 4.1, at the end of this chapter, lists various videotext tests underway in the U.S.

EARLY U.S. DEVELOPMENTS

While some U.S. companies such as RCA began tinkering with videotext in the early 1970s, U.S. officials generally left the British, French and Canadians to do the technological spadework. It wasn't until June 1978, several years after the British Broadcasting Corporation (BBC) had developed CEEFAX, that the first American broadcast teletext experiment got underway, sponsored by Bonneville International Corp.'s KSL-TV in Salt Lake City. Nearly four years later, KSL was still transmitting teletext to 12 obsolete decoders made by Texas Instruments using a modified Ceefax teletext system. A KSL official admitted that the test was "dormant," that technical feasibility had been established, but that no substantial market research had been done. KSL preferred the British system to the Canadian one because of its lower costs. Although its initial test was all but dead, Bonneville announced early in 1982 that it would use Zenith hardware in a new test with its Seattle TV station.

The Standards Issue

Bonneville's very cautious approach to videotext development was almost the opposite of CBS' approach. CBS, the first of the nation's major TV networks to become involved with videotext, tried both the French and

British systems simultaneously, beginning in 1979. CBS decided to cast its lot with the French Antiope system, because the graphics were superior and could be easily expanded, and aggressively began lobbying at the federal level for adoption of a modified Antiope teletext standard. Then, in mid-1981, the company decided to join AT&T's videotext camp after the French and Canadians had pronounced themselves in favor of the AT&T approach for North America. Late in 1982, CBS will run a viewdata test in Ridgewood, NJ in a joint effort with AT&T (which had elected CBS president Thomas Wyman to its board of directors earlier in the year). NBC and Westinghouse announced teletext tests in 1981. In June 1982 both CBS and NBC said they would make teletext services available to all affiliates by early in 1983, the first major broadcasters to make a system-wide commitment to teletext. Whether CBS and NBC affiliates will clamor for the service remains to be seen. NBC, which had been sharing an Antiope system with CBS in a test with that network in Los Angeles, also announced its support of the North American videotext display standard.

Most U.S. videotext proponents have chosen sides and are moving forward with their own strategic plans despite the lack of formal videotext regulations. The Videotex Industry Association was formed in fall 1981 by representatives of all major videotext factions, such as the North American standard backers, the British, the French and Canadians. Throughout 1981 and 1982 consulting groups were prognosticating, books were written and videotext information in the form of reports, trade shows, magazines and newsletters proliferated.

Videotext and the Communications Industry

By 1981 and early 1982, a landmark period in the development of videotext, major U.S. companies in nearly all communications fields had tested some form of videotext or announced major field trials. Among them were AT&T, CBS, NBC, Westinghouse, Field Enterprises, Time Inc., Times Mirror, Knight-Ridder, Zenith, Cox Communications and Oak Industries. The nation's top wire services—the Associated Press, United Press International, Dow Jones, Reuters—were delivering information to cable TV systems by satellite using a British-style teletext system. The nation's top newspaper chain, Knight-Ridder, had conducted one viewdata test, sold the results to several other news chains and announced a product rollout for 1983. Every major communications delivery system, including multipoint distribution service (MDS), a microwave common carrier service, had been used to deliver text to TV screens.

The interest of print and electronic publishers in new delivery systems comes at a time when both industries have reached maturity. Newspaper circulation is nearly stagnant while network audience shares are beginning to decline, partly because of the rapid growth of cable and subscription TV services. Broadcasters and publishers alike see new delivery systems both as a threat to their traditional products and as pathways to nontraditional markets—a way for newspaper companies to reach people who only watch TV and a way for broadcasters to reach people who only read newspapers. Broadcasters and print publishers are already integrated to a certain degree. Major print and broadcast companies such as Time Inc., Times Mirror, Cox Communications and Dow Jones have their corporate feet planted firmly in both territories.

Cable TV companies have joined the videotext race because they see videotext as an attractive franchising feature which can be used to convince city and state officials of the company's resolve to provide a "state of the art" system. But the cable TV industry, still riding the crest of a seemingly insatiable demand for video entertainment, continues to view videotext as a source of revenue only after subscriber fees, ad-supported entertainment services and home security systems.

Regulations and Teletext

One of the major issues facing the teletext industry is how the vertical blanking interval (VBI) will be regulated. Who, for instance, owns the VBI? What can be done with it? Will teletext programming be subject to standard broadcast rules such as the Fairness Doctrine? The FCC may set rules by the fall of 1982, but until then, a regulatory vacuum is being filled partly by court decisions.

The first major conflict in 1981 involved federal copyright rules over which the FCC has no jurisdiction. The debate was between WGN Continental Broadcasting Co., a subsidiary of the Tribune Co., and United Video, Inc., a common carrier. WGN, testing transmission of teletext not only to Chicago, but via a satellite transponder controlled by United Video, to an affiliated cable TV system in Albuquerque, NM, sued United Video when the latter stripped WGN's teletext programming, news and TV schedules from the satellite feed, substituting another teletext service, Dow Jones Cable News, for distribution to cable TV systems.

A federal district court judge dismissed the WGN complaint late in 1981 saying that United Video was exempt from copyright liability because of its status as a passive common carrier, but a three judge federal appeals panel overturned that ruling, backing WGN's claim that its teletext service was directly related to its news program and thus part of a single copyrighted work which United Video could not legally alter. (If WGN had copyrighted its teletext programming separately, the appeals court noted,

United Video could legally transmit only the video portion of the WGN broadcast.) The appeals panel made clear, however, that its decision did not grant WGN an ownership claim on the vertical blanking interval.

The Role of AT&T

One of the most significant influences on the development of videotext in the U.S. will be AT&T. The company signaled its interest in this technology first by its electronic directory assistance trial in Albany, NY which began in August 1979 and then by participating with Knight-Ridder Newspapers, Inc. in the Viewtron viewdata test in Coral Gables, FL. AT&T boosted its investment in videotext substantially in 1981 when it unveiled its Presentation Level Protocol display standard and then announced a viewdata field trial with CBS scheduled to begin in fall 1982. (See CBS profile later in this chapter.)

Early in 1982, as the result of protracted antitrust litigation and possibly because of Congressional legislative activity, AT&T and the Justice Department agreed on a restructuring of the company in exchange for an end to the litigation. The restructuring was approved with key modifications, late in August 1982. One modification to the settlement will bar AT&T from new electronic publishing ventures for at least seven years. But AT&T will be allowed to continue existing information services and Yellow Pages publishing. While the settlement bars the company from major new information publishing activities, AT&T will still be free to provide information publishers with equipment and communications lines for information distribution.

The agreement will force AT&T to give up its local operating companies, but will keep the new independent operating companies out of information publishing. AT&T will be allowed to buy and operate cable TV systems, but AT&T officials have all but promised to stay out of information production or traditional cable TV services (probably to stem the criticism that followed announcement of the antitrust settlement and Congressional attempts to impose new restrictions on the company.)

Organization of a new AT&T without its local operating units has not been completed, although the Long Lines, Western Electric and Bell Labs arms of the company will undoubtedly survive in some form as part of the parent company. The Western Electric equipment-making company is designing and manufacturing the home information terminals for the CBS videotext test in New Jersey. AT&T also unveiled a frame creation system designed to support its proposed videotext standard. The display generator, announced at a videotext trade show in mid-1982, includes a monitor, keyboard, dual floppy disc drives and a graphics tablet with stylus to allow freehand drawing. The system is expected to sell for about $34,000. The first customer for the terminals was Knight-Ridder Newspaper's Viewdata Corp. of America subsidiary.

The first unregulated company to be formed by AT&T (not in connection with the antitrust settlement, but as the result of FCC efforts to both deregulate telecommunications industries and stimulate competition) was American Bell, a data communications company which began operation on July 1, 1982. The company planned to offer a communications network that would allow normally incompatible computer terminals to communicate with each other.

One Standard or Many?

Four years after CBS and KSL began dipping their corporate toes into videotext, major communications industry trade groups are still unwilling to decide which system is the best. Some continue to insist that government authorities should make that choice and appoint one technology as *the* system for the U.S. The FCC has resisted efforts to lock the U.S. into a single videotext standard despite the claims that manufacturers need the encouragement of a standard to begin large scale production of videotext equipment.

The jury is still out regarding how videotext will be regulated although current trends are toward minimum regulation. In October 1981, the FCC initiated a formal rule-making procedure. "We believe it is important to provide a regulatory environment that is conducive to the emergence and implementation of new technology and new uses of the [radio] spectrum."[2] The FCC's favored "open environment"[3] was the economic equivalent of the law of the jungle. If the FCC proposal is adopted by the agency, none of the beasts in the teletext jungle will be granted special status although all may have to abide by a broad technical and policy framework which might create a zoo without cages.

At the time of printing, the FCC had not officially adopted the "open environment" approach, but comments filed in connection with the proceeding involved little that hadn't been said before the rule-making was initiated. Trade groups such as the Electronic Industries Association (EIA) and the National Association of Broadcasters (NAB) continued to insist that a single teletext standard was needed to encourage manufacturers to produce teletext equipped TV sets. Their claims were largely discredited, however, when Zenith Radio Corp., one of two leading U.S. television set manufacturers, told the FCC it didn't need any special encouragement to make teletext decoders, only a clear signal from the marketplace. The Videotex Industry Association (VIA), like other trade groups involved with videotext, refuses to take sides in the standards debate although its president is a leading advocate of the North American standard.

Without a national or even an industry-wide commitment to one videotext system, many have emerged, and all the major systems are being tested by at least one major U.S. communications company. Unlike the tests that started in 1978, the current wave of experimentation is designed to answer crucial marketing rather than technical questions. The leading questions are no longer: Will it work, and if so, how well? Today's videotext experimenters are convinced that videotext technology will work. Now U.S. companies are more interested in how they can transform videotext products (many of which originated abroad), into profit-making services for domestic customers. What do consumers want from a videotext system—games? advice? news? book reviews? bank statements? merchandise catalogs? What kinds of graphics and response times are required to make the services palatable? What will consumers pay for such systems and how should a company go about reaching potential customers? Should companies develop telephone-based systems, cable TV systems or broadcast teletext systems? These are the questions American companies are confronting. Many may learn enough over the next two years to answer the key questions of videotext — if it will succeed, and if so, in what forms.

PROFILES OF SELECTED COMPANIES
INVOLVED WITH VIDEOTEXT

CBS, INC.
51 W. 52 St.
New York, NY 10019

CBS, Inc. has been the most active of the three major broadcast networks in exploring video technology. While CBS is one of the largest book and magazine publishers in the U.S., the company has made significant research and/or development commitments to every video delivery technology—broadcast TV, cable TV, videotext, video cassette, video disc and satellite broadcasting. Involvement in producing entertainment and information services as well as the delivery systems puts CBS in control of the so-called communications "pipelines" and the products sent to consumers through those pipelines.

Although it may not be the most advanced of the videotext pioneers, CBS is certainly far ahead of its major broadcast rivals in developing videotext tests and services. Involvement with videotext began in 1979, shortly after the KSL-TV experiment started. CBS tested both the British and French teletext systems at its St. Louis TV station KMOX.

Support of the French System

CBS announced its support of a modified version of the French video-text system in the summer of 1980, while the EIA was still grappling with the standards issue. CBS cited the French system's flexibility in choosing an Antiope-like videotext proposal, claiming that the Telidon system, not directly tested by CBS, would be too expensive for widespread consumer acceptance. A CBS official later said, however, that CBS thought "the French system is the best because it's the most extensible and it can be made compatible with the Canadian system." Compatibility with the Canadian system came shortly thereafter when AT&T announced in May 1981 its so-called North American videotext display standard which would allow the French and Canadian systems to co-exist under certain circumstances.

According to *Science* magazine, CBS and other broadcasters were using the videotext standards debate to delay the development of teletext, perhaps fearing the service would threaten advertising revenues. But CBS insisted at the time that it wasn't testing teletext out of fear. "We don't see it as a threatening technology," explained Harry Smith, vice president for technology. "Our whole business is based on providing a service to the public. I guess we figure that teletext improves the total service that we can provide."[4]

Videotext Field Trials

CBS made it clear that the company was serious about videotext in November 1980, when it announced a $1 million field trial at its KNXT affiliate in Los Angeles. The trial was conducted in conjunction with public broadcasting station KCET-TV and the Caption Center of WGBH-TV in Boston. CBS said the Los Angeles trial would not be a technical one and was expected to involve a total of 100 test sites. "We know that it works," said one CBS official, "It's a question of what we can do with it." Perishable information such as traffic information, weather reports and advertising were expected to play major roles in the test. "One thing we want to find out," said a KNXT official, "is whether there is an appetite for it in the business and commercial communities."

(As an illustration of CBS' seriousness in developing new pipelines into the home, it persuaded the FCC to waive a ban on network ownership of cable systems. It then filed an application for the 27,000-home Alameda, CA cable franchise, saying it would continue to develop cable text services such as North American Newstime, The Weather Channel, ABC-Westinghouse's Satellite Newschannels and Reuter's Interactive Data Retrieval service. Then early in 1982, CBS announced the acquisition of a two year old 35-channel cable system near Dallas from American Family Corp. for more than $14 million.)

Soon after winning approval of the cable cross-ownership waiver, CBS announced it would conduct a viewdata test in Ridgewood, NJ beginning in fall 1982 and lasting for seven months. Communications facilities, computers and home terminals will be supplied by AT&T. Announcement of the test came before the proposed Justice Department/AT&T settlement splitting up the phone company and permitting it to enter new businesses. CBS emphasized that it "will be solely responsible for all of the information content in the test."

The test will take place in an "upscale" community and involve two groups of 100 homes, each of which will have videotext equipment and services for about three months. Information and transaction services will be tried, along with advertising. "This test is an important component of the $40 to $50 million annual development spending announced by CBS president Thomas Wyman in February 1981," Smith said, although he declined to say specifically how much CBS is investing in the test. CBS had already participated as an information provider in several videotext tests, including the Viewtron test in Florida and the Dow Jones-Sammons videotext test near Dallas.

Satellite Delivery Systems

While CBS is undoubtedly spending millions to develop its teletext and videotext trials, the company's biggest gamble may be in the field of satellite delivery systems. The company quietly acquired two transponders on Satcom IV, a communications satellite owned and operated by RCA, late in 1981. The going rate for similar transponders was more than $10 million each at the time of the sale although terms were not disclosed and the legality of the sale itself is still questionable. The transponders could be used to deliver teletext to CBS affiliates or for other informational services.

COMPUSERVE INFORMATION SERVICE
5000 Arlington Centre Blvd.
Columbus, OH 43220

The CompuServe Information Service (CIS) began in 1979 as MicroNET, the outgrowth of a computer services company which had been serving corporate and government clients with a variety of problem solving programs. CompuServe Inc., the parent company of CIS, first launched MicroNET as an off-hours service aimed partially at making use of computer power that was unused. Initial services included personal finance programs and an electronic message service. Users paid $5 per connect hour for hooking their terminals into the CompuServe proprietary telephone network. Presently, it offers its customers a variety of information and transaction services such as electronically delivered newsletters, electronic mail and bulletin board services that allow customers to communicate with each other, news from Associated Press, and the Comp-U-Star shopping service. The company also provides raw computing power and programs that can be downloaded to a customer's terminal from CompuServe's mainframes, including video games.

Prior to the launching of MicroNET late in 1978, a merger plan proposing the absorption of CompuServe by H&R Block was revealed. H&R Block paid $22.8 million for CompuServe, nearly 14 times the company's earnings. The merger became effective in May 1980. Block's 1981 (year ending April 30, 1982) revenues were $318.7 million with earnings of $38.3 million prior to the acquisition. CompuServe's 1981 revenues totaled $27.6 million with earnings of $2.34 million. Block said "synergy between CompuServe's computer technology and H&R Block's tax preparation business was not a primary consideration for the acquisition." It said that CompuServe's telecommunications network, software library and management made the acquisition attractive.

Shortly after the CompuServe-Block merger, CompuServe announced major expansion moves including a retailing agreement with Tandy Corp., parent company of Radio Shack, the nation's largest chain of consumer computer retail outlets. The move made CIS available nationwide and was later expanded to include Canadian Radio Shack stores. CompuServe also announced that an electronic edition of the *Columbus Dispatch* would be made available to customers along with 11 other Associated Press newspapers, including *The New York Times* and the *Washington Post*.

CompuServe formally announced exploration of new distribution systems in August 1980 in conjunction with Warner Amex Cable Communications and Warner Communications' Atari home computer division. The test, using Warner Amex's Columbus, OH two-way cable system instead of phone lines to connect customers to CIS, didn't begin until late 1980. A year later Warner-Amex senior vice president and chief scientist John Fisher was openly skeptical about the project. Only 15 computers were hooked up to CIS as of early 1982, although the test was originally supposed to involve at least 100 terminals. Individual rather than household usage was to be tracked during a second phase of the test. Fisher said, "I just don't think the ASCII keyboard is the answer." Text only doesn't work well, he explained, and graphics are costly to generate. A CompuServe spokesman said his company was more pleased with the test: "Our goal was to develop the technology (for cable transmission). That has been done very nicely."

A doubter of the value of home computers, Fisher said Warner Amex's interest in information services, rather than entertainment services, came from the American Express side of the joint venture. He noted that Warner Amex's Qube two-way cable system was developed for urban markets where movies and sporting events would not produce enough revenue to justify expensive construction of a cable plant. Qube was designed to make urban markets profitable by offering a range of nontraditional cable delivered services. It also was intended to begin a purchase-on-impulse system that would allow subscribers to buy both video programming and other merchandise from their living rooms without making a telephone call, going to a store or mailing an order form. Usage of the Atari terminals dropped off considerably after the novelty had diminished, according to Fisher.

In mid-1981 CompuServe began enlisting major cable TV companies to support further development of the cable distribution system. The service was tentatively called INFOChannel. A CompuServe official said cable distribution would permit faster data transmission with lower error rates. By early 1982 INFOChannel had made little progress. CompuServe senior vice president George Minot acknowledged that no significant financial commitments had been made by cable systems and that potential makers of home terminals were having enough trouble developing the long promised addressable cable converters to think seriously about developing home terminals that would bring CIS to users via cable. By late 1981 and early 1982, CIS was regularly being included in cable TV franchise bids, although cable distribution was still being tested only in Columbus, OH.

By mid-July 1981, CIS had passed its top rival, The Source, with about 12,000 paying users. It was still being used primarily by computer hobbyists, but business use of the service was a growing component. Daytime use of CIS was first offered to customers on November 1, 1980 at $22.50 per connect hour.

A two-year experiment in videotext journalism involving the Associated Press (AP), 10 newspapers and CompuServe ended June 30, 1982. With the experiment's conclusion, only three newspapers are continuing to provide CompuServe with electronic information. All parties seem to have agreed that the experiment was educational for the information providers, but that the market for electronic newspapers is not here yet. Richard Hochhauser, president of RMH Research, Inc., which monitored the experiment for AP, said, "In general, videotext has a future, but it may depend on a lot more than technology, including the growth of homes willing and able to use it. You have to have enough homes with computers. That does not exist today."

By late 1983, CompuServe had built its CIS customer base to more than 75,000, far ahead of The Source. Like its rival, though, CIS became increasingly business-oriented, adding services such as Commodities News Service and financial newsletters. Undoubtedly the single biggest stimulus to the growth in customers, however, has been the personal computer boom. By offering trial subscriptions to new computer owners, CompuServe has greatly broadened its reach.

DOW JONES & CO. INC.
22 Cortlandt St.
New York, NY 10007

Dow Jones & Co. Inc. began its first videotext service, then known as Dow Jones News/Recall and later called News/Retrieval, as a joint venture with Bunker Ramo Corp. in 1973. Its primary customers were stockbrokers and banks who used custom-made video display terminals or teleprinters to retrieve items from the *Wall Street Journal*, *Barron*'s and the Dow Jones News Service, also known as the broadtape. According to Dow Jones, the service became profitable in 1976. By the end of 1977 the News/Retrieval service had more than 2500 customers for a new, lower-cost version, which utilized standard data terminals and provided stock quotations.

Growth of the News/Retrieval Service

Dow Jones bought Bunker Ramo's share of the News/Retrieval operation in May 1979. By the end of 1980 News/Retrieval had 15,000 customers and was billing itself as "the world's largest news-on-demand supplier." Dow Jones also joined with the Associated Press (AP) and Telerate to market computer-delivered stock quotations to European and Asian customers.

By the end of 1983, News/Retrieval had 100,000 customers and was growing by more than 5000 per month. Customers in the brokerage community are served by distributors like Bunker Ramo, who have complex package prices for quotation and retrieval services. Those customers served by Dow Jones directly—including personal computer owners—pay between $9 and $72 per hour, depending on time of day and specific information required.

Dow Jones began major new undertakings in 1980 and 1981 aimed at using new delivery systems to broaden its market potential. In its first major effort to capture the consumer market it tested News/Retrieval distribution by cable TV in Irving, TX, to selected residents of a wealthy housing development. Another test in a Dallas suburb involving a major cable TV company, Merrill Lynch & Co., and A.H. Belo Corp. was announced in May 1980. Dow Jones was an information provider for several videotext tests sponsored by other companies, including the Knight-Ridder/AT&T Viewtron test in Coral Gables, FL.

Other Developments

Early in 1981 Dow Jones joined with Knight-Ridder in an unsuccessful bid to acquire one of the nation's largest cable TV companies, UA-Columbia Cablevision. (Dow Jones settled instead for a 24.5% interest in another large cable system, Continental Cablevision.) Dow Jones did team up with Prime Cable Corp. and a group which controls the Princeton Packet newspaper to acquire two small cable franchises in southern New Jersey. The resulting system promises to deliver a variety of information services, both one-and two-way, to Princeton area residents via a 110-channel cable system.

Later in 1981, the company began delivering local and financial information to Danbury, CT area cable TV subscribers using an Antiope teletext system and a channel leased from the local cable operator. In 1981 Dow Jones also began a one-way, text-only news service for cable TV subscribers.

As the population of personal computers soared in 1981, 1982 and 1983, Dow Jones began extending its data base offerings, adding UPI weather summaries in 1981; sports, movie reviews and an online encyclopedia in 1982. In 1983 it announced an agreement to provide access for its customers to a new electronic mail service being launched by MCI. In 1982, Dow Jones also began publishing microcomputer software packages, e.g., in investment analysis and portfolio management, an obvious complement to the News/Retrieval service. By marketing DJN/R as a tie-in for new personal computer owners, Dow Jones succeeded in reaching that segment of the consumer population that is most disposed to use electronic information services.

FIELD ENTERPRISES
401 North Wabash Ave.
Chicago, IL 60611

Field Enterprises, Inc., a privately held communications conglomerate based in Chicago, formally entered the teletext field in January 1981. WFLD-TV, Field's television station in Chicago, received permission from the Federal Communications Commission (FCC) to conduct the nation's first commercial teletext trial: i.e., one that would involve charges to host sites and advertisers. Field set up a new subsidiary, Field Electronic Publishing (FEP), to conduct the test.

Field adopted the British teletext system with technical specifications identical to those filed on March 26, 1981 with the FCC by the United Kingdom Teletext Industry Group. Economics—cheaper decoders—and flexibility were the major reasons given by Field officials for their selection of the British teletext system. They also noted that the system had been tested extensively and that 300,000 decoder units were already in use. Although Field supports the British system as a U.S. standard, the emergence of a non-compatible AT&T-backed standard proposal may have prompted Field officials to say in September 1981 that they doubted the need for a single teletext standard.

KEYFAX service began on April 30, 1981, but by September of that year only 25 of the 100 authorized decoders were in the field. The company said originally that most of the decoding units would be placed in public or private areas with high circulation to maximize research opportunities. Field officials later said 75% of the decoders would be placed in bars, restaurants, hospitals and transportation terminals, and 25% in private homes.

Zenith Radio Corp., aligned initially with the British teletext system but vowing to follow consumer preferences in teletext hardware, manufactured the Field decoding units. Field also made extensive use of the British expertise, using Logica software and some BBC-supplied reference information.

At the heart of the KEYFAX system are Digital Equipment Corp. PDP 11/34 computers owned by the Chicago *Sun-Times*, a Field-owned newspaper, and Atex text processing equipment. Control Data 80 megabyte disc drives serve as long-term storage devices for the Atex system.

The machinery yields a display on user terminals of 24 lines per screen, 42 characters per line—about 70 to 85 words per frame. One hundred frames of information are available to the user at any given time. Maximum response time for any frame, once requested, is 25 seconds; the average is 12 seconds.

Information providers in addition to the *Sun-Times* included the Associated Press, United Press International, Dow Jones, the Chicago Public Library and the Chicago City News Bureau. The 100 frame KEYFAX magazine contains five categories each with its own index frame —news, sports, finance-business, weather-traffic and entertainment.

Although private homes paid nothing for KEYFAX, other host sites were charged up to $100 per month to lease decoders. The small number of sites involved made the test less than attractive as an advertising vehicle, except for experimentation purposes. But early in September 1981 Field took a major step toward alleviating that problem by sending an adapted form of KEYFAX to WFLD viewers in decoderless form from midnight to 6 a.m., hours that the station had not been using. The importance of advertising was underscored not only by Field's NITE OWL service, but by the elevation of *Sun-Times* classified ad manager Donald Kaleta to the presidency of FEP shortly before NITE OWL went on the air.

NITE OWL is reportedly attracting 35,000 to 75,000 viewers nightly, and reaches nearly three million homes. British videotext marketers say Field has attracted 11 advertisers paying $13,650 for a 13-week deal, $10,020 for seven weeks, $1800 for one week and $300 per night. A 20-second spot averages $8.33 on a 13-week contract.

NITE OWL's debut apparently marked the first time a major U.S. TV station had set aside a major block of time for text only. NITE OWL consists of a 20-minute cycle including 60 frames, each frame appearing for 20 seconds. About 25% of all frames is devoted to advertising. News, sports and weather are included in each cycle, accompanied by background music which could be used to voice over text in the future. Business, leisure activities and special features play a secondary role in the cycle. KEYFAX journalists produce NITE OWL, thus adding little to capital or manpower expenses while offering advertisers access to one of the nation's top TV markets. Field officials also note that putting text on commercial TV may get consumers used to the idea of receiving text via their TV sets, perhaps as a prelude to a commercial launch of KEYFAX.

After nearly a year of testing KEYFAX, Field was apparently encouraged enough to start a commercial, national teletext service, but not confident enough to bear all of the risk. The company announced a joint venture with Satellite Syndicated Systems (SSS) in March 1982 aimed at delivering a commercial, satellite-delivered teletext service to consumers by November 1982. SSS is a privately held communications company which develops commercial video programs, operates subscription TV and cable TV systems and transmits programming to cable TV operators by satellite. Some of those services are text only (e.g., the Dow Jones and Reuters news services for cable systems) and are delivered in the vertical blanking interval of the WTBS video signal which SSS distributes to cable operators by satellite. Cable systems use British style teletext decoders made by Zenith to strip the news services from the WTBS signal and then relay the service by cable to their cable TV subscribers.

As of July 1982, pricing for the service had not been set but a monthly subscription fee, a decoder lease or purchase charge and advertising are all expected to be part of the service's revenue picture.

About six weeks after announcing the proposed joint venture with SSS, Field decided to take a back seat to Centel Corp. and Honeywell Inc. in a new videotext venture that is expected to absorb KEYFAX and develop a commercial viewdata service similar to Viewtron. The new company, KEYCOM, was expected to spend more than $20 million during the two years following its formation in April 1982 to continue development of KEYFAX and a viewdata service based on the so-called North American display standard. The viewdata service, KEYTRAN, was expected to be offered initially in the Chicago area by mid-1983 for less than $25 per month. This would also include the lease of a Honeywell-made home terminal which would be connected to the subscriber's TV set and telephone. Honeywell mainframe computers will be the host machines for the service.

Field officials would not say directly why they gave up their leading role in developing KEYFAX. In 1981 the company began talks aimed at acquiring a major cable TV systems operator. Those negotiations collapsed in mid-1982, but Field then announced plans to sell off its group of television stations with proceeds to be invested in cable television. The shift in corporate focus and the apparent desire of Field to make a major investment in cable TV may have discouraged the company from plowing major sums into the development of KEYFAX. Development of a viewdata service would have also required development of expertise in a new technology.

KNIGHT-RIDDER NEWSPAPERS INC.
One Herald Plaza
Miami, FL 33101

Knight-Ridder Newspapers Inc., the nation's largest newspaper chain as measured by total daily circulation, with more than $1 billion in annual revenues, announced its intention to explore the concept of viewdata on April 17, 1979. The announcement was made by president Alvah Chapman Jr. at the company's annual shareholders' meeting.

In 1978 and 1979 when Knight-Ridder executives visited England to examine the Prestel videotext system, the company became a temporary information provider for Prestel. Knight-Ridder officials learned the basics of data base design, but felt that U.S. consumer attitudes could not be projected from the British experience. "We concluded that the only way to learn about U.S. consumer attitudes was to build a prototype system, place it in U.S. homes and conduct extensive research," a Knight-Ridder official said at the Viewdata '81 conference in London in October 1981.

Viewtron—the Coral Gables Test

Late in 1978, Knight-Ridder agreed to co-sponsor a videotext test with AT&T. After pre-testing the system by installing terminals in employees' homes—so-called "friendly" sites—the companies proceeded to place terminals in other homes in Coral Gables, FL, a wealthy Miami suburb. Knight-Ridder supplied the host computer and information; AT&T the communications lines and home terminals. Testing of Viewtron in non-friendly homes began on July 14, 1980, ultimately involving 204 homes and 691 individual users.

Specially adapted TV sets allowed users in their homes to be connected to a computer in Miami via dedicated telephone lines. Viewtron permitted access to about 18,000 frames of information at any one time. Frames were selected by the viewer using a special keypad similar to a calculator. Users could search the data base by an alphabetic subject index, by keywords or by a special category index with 15 headings. Available to users of Viewtron were continually updated news, weather, sports, stock market reports, interactive shopping, banking, travel and entertainment schedules, learning aids, games, quizzes, consumer advice and energy saving tips.

The modified British display system allowed IPs and advertisers to use 16 colors and a screen which could handle 20 lines of 40 characters each. IPs for the test included Knight-Ridder's Miami newspaper, *The Miami Herald*, Consumer's Union, the American Cancer Society, Macmillan Publishing Co., Inc., The New York Times Co., Dow Jones & Co. Inc., HP Books, Associated Press, *Congressional Quarterly,* Addison-Wesley, Universal Press Syndicate, CBS Publications, United Media Enterprises and United Press International. Advertisers were: Eastern Airlines, Sears Roebuck & Co., B. Dalton Booksellers, Grand Union, Co., Southeast Banking Corp., Official Airline Guides, Inc., AAA World Wide Travel Agency, J.C. Penney Co., Inc., Shell Oil Corp., Spec's Music Co., Service Merchandise Corp., Cousins Associates, Realtors, Shell's City Liquors, Master Host Dinner Service, Merrill Lynch, Jordan Marsh Tickets, S&H Green Stamps and Direct Mail Marketing Association.

Fourteen months and $2 million after the test began, Knight-Ridder shut down the Coral Gables project. But three months before the end, Knight-Ridder announced a new beginning. Broadcasting president Albert Gillen said the company would undertake a full market trial of a revamped Viewtron somewhere in southern Florida beginning in 1983. Gillen said Viewtron would require fees from both users and advertisers in the 1983 test and expected to involve 5000 subscribers within its first year of operation. The data base is expected to be at least four times the size of the original Viewtron information bank. Knight-Ridder also announced its support of the AT&T North American videotext display standard.

Results of the Test

What did Knight-Ridder find that was so encouraging? The company regards most of the data it collected during the Coral Gables test as proprietary, but company officials do say the following:

- consumers said they liked Viewtron, would find the system useful in their homes and the majority would be willing to pay for the service;

- usage was close to company expectations, often running as high as 30 to 60 minutes per day per household;

- users weren't intimidated by the hardware;

- electronic messaging was a "key strength" of the system; and

- two-way shopping and banking had very strong appeal (some users ordered more than $200 worth of merchandise through Viewtron in 30 days or less).

The Associated Press may have accounted for the single largest block of usage among all the information and service providers and advertisers—about one-eighth of all system usage, more than half of all news frames requested. News frames accounted for about 25% of all Viewtron usage based on data gathered during the first six months of the test.

Users in 115 homes that had Viewtron service for four weeks viewed an average of 15 AP frames daily, but 10 homes that had the service for six months viewed about 13 frames daily, perhaps indicating that a novelty factor makes for higher initial usage. According to AP, national news, Middle East reports and stock listings were the most frequently requested information categories. (The test results may have been skewed by the presidential election campaign and the Iranian hostage crisis.) AP found that usage of its frames was slightly lower as the income of the user increased, and that those viewers 19 and older used Viewtron more in four week test homes while those under 19 used the system more frequently in the six month test homes.

A two week study of 29 homes in January 1981 found that 43% of users ordered the last page of any story that was started and that short stories were more likely to be completed than long ones, although longer stories were started more frequently. Stories completed most often were sports scores, political stories and death notices.

Commercial Launch

When Viewtron was finally offered to paying customers in November 1983, Knight-Ridder was charging $12 per month for hours of usage. In addition, customers paid estimated telephone charges of $14 per month, and had to buy a terminal from AT&T for $600 (regular price was to be $900).

Having spent $18 million on Viewtron before the commercial launch, Knight-Ridder was committed to another $8 million for a year of service. Its target was to sign up 5000 or more customers in the first 12 months. On the basis of preliminary financial plans, Knight-Ridder officials hope to have Viewtron in the black four or five years after the startup. However, uncertainty regarding the ultimate profitability of the venture was signaled by Knight-Ridder chairman Alvah Chapman Jr. at the company's 1982 annual meeting when he said that the computers associated with the project could be sold or used elsewhere in the company "in the event we should decide not to go ahead with the project."

THE SOURCE TELECOMPUTING CORP.
1616 Anderson Rd.
McLean, VA 22102

"By mid-year, we'll be in the home like Tupperware," Jack Taub told the *Wall Street Journal* early in 1980. President of Telecomputing Corp. of America (TCA) at the time, Taub said he wanted to have 100,000 customers for his remote computing and information service by the end of 1980. Two years later, Taub was gone, TCA had been acquired by Reader's Digest Association Inc. and was less than a quarter of the way to its 1980 goal, and the Digest was looking for a partner to help finance the company's growth.

Early Developments

TCA started as a private company in early 1979 with 35 employees and a general interest electronic data bank. The Source then was a computer terminal and $100 away from anyone interested. Off peak usage charges were $2.75 per hour. By early 1982 the company had 120 employees, computer terminals were cheaper, and the service had been expanded to include more information, communications and transaction services. But the initial $100 subscription fee remains and a $10 per month monthly minimum has been added. The cheapest hourly rate, from midnight to 7 a.m., is $4.25.

Now known as Source Telecomputing Corp. (STC), The Source had about 20,000 paying customers by mid-1982. Midway through 1981, the company formally abandoned its initial target market in favor of a more monied clientele, mainly businessmen who had computers in their homes.

STC officials admit that The Source's first two years were rocky ones. Customers threatened a boycott in mid-1980 after a price increase. An information supplier complained that the company was slow to pay for the information it bought. Dealer relations were poor. When Reader's Digest stepped in to take over the financially ailing company in October 1980, a legal fracas between TCA principals broke out, temporarily delaying completion of the $10 million sale. During the first half of 1982 several key

Source executives left The Source, including chief executive officer Graeme Keeping and president Marshall Graham. George Grune, Digest vice president and director, took over as chief executive officer although he was not expected to be a full time Source official. Source spokesmen wouldn't say specifically why Keeping and Graham left but insisted that it was a mutual agreement. The newest Source regime features a pared down executive staff emphasizing team decision-making.

A year after the sale, STC executives felt secure enough to invite key trade press representatives to the company's Virginia headquarters for a day-long press conference and demonstration. "We have a long, long way to go," one official said of STC's relations with its dealers. But STC's new parent company is apparently willing to finance major projects to improve The Source—$250,000, for instance, to print and distribute 35,000 new user guides for customers and dealers. (The guides are free to subscribers.) When the Digest took over The Source, the service was operating on two computers that could handle a maximum of 60 users simultaneously. By late 1981, STC had six computers and could handle 304 users at one time. A new operating system to be added late in 1982 is expected to decrease response time and lower operating costs.

A Shift in Emphasis

While computer hobbyists were the first Source customers, STC discovered through a survey conducted in May 1981 that its customer base had shifted. The survey showed that 42% of the users were businessmen, 16% scientists and engineers, 14% computer science workers and 12% engaged in other professional occupations. Less than 30% belonged to a computer club. The average age of survey respondents was 38 and average annual income was $50,000. (Fifteen percent said they made more than $80,000 annually.) Most users were male and held degrees above the baccalaureate level.

STC's response to the survey was to include more business oriented information like Stockvue, Management Contents and Commodity News Services. A new, more expensive tier of services was added called Source Plus. But STC also announced forays into other areas. The company is working with a unit of Cox Communications to send a one-way, 16-line by 32-character display format information service to Cox Cable subscribers in San Diego as part of Cox's interactive Indax cable service. Several major cable companies in addition to Cox were also offering some form of The Source in their franchise bids. Cable TV companies offer The Source a major new and growing market consisting of more than 24 million cable TV subscribers as of mid-1982.

Source officials are also developing new services for current customers including several different communications services and a yellow pages-type directory of major metropolitan areas. Plans to make a full text encyclopedia available were being reconsidered in mid-1982. Advertising is also being explored, although The Source has no graphic capabilities yet.

Former STC chairman Graeme Keeping noted that most Source users don't use the service in a given month, despite the minimum monthly charge. Yet, prime time usage had increased rapidly to 42% during the last half of 1981. That trend may signify greater use of the service at work rather than at home.

TIME INC.
Time & Life Bldg.
New York, NY 10020

Time Inc.'s video division is that company's fastest growing sector and is expected to surpass print publishing in 1982 as a source of profits. Much of this growth in video was through the acquisition of American Television and Communications Corp., (ATC) one of the largest cable television system operators in the U.S. and through Home Box Office and Cinemax, two major premium cable services. Time owns one-third of the USA Cable Network (with Paramount Pictures Corporation and MCA, Inc.); WOTV (Grand Rapids, MI); and Time-Life Video, a producer and distributor of video training programs. In August 1982 Time announced that it will start a magazine for cable and pay television subscribers, called *TV-Cable Week*.

As of December 1981, ATC operated 125 cable systems in 33 states, with more than 1.8 million subscribers, and ATC is actively exploring new cable-delivered services, such as home security and home information systems. A growing number of ATC systems are engaged in joint ventures with local newspapers to provide news on ad-supported channels. New businesses that require two-way communications capability, such as banking and shopping, will be developed more gradually, according to Time Inc.

A Projected National Teletext Service

Already a giant in magazine publishing and in cable, Time plans to test a 24-hour satellite-delivered national teletext "magazine" using ATC-owned cable systems in Orlando, FL and San Diego, CA as local distribution loops. (San Diego is also the site of Cox Cable's Indax interactive service.)

When first announced, Time's teletext project, to use Telidon technology because of its superior graphics capability, was described as "the first national multichannel teletext service designed for in home use." Two hundred users in each city will be supplied with numeric keypads which they will use to select frames of information from a base of up to 5000 frames. No charges will be levied initially; if the test is successful, Time may launch the service on a national basis.

Emphasis on Content

Time is concentrating more on the content than on the technology and network. Sean McCarthy, director of Time's video group development unit, said Time "will try to play in the content world" with its teletext project, much as it has been active in supplying programming for cable television. Time has about 60 people working on the service, and has been testing its editorial product in New York using 1000 people in focus groups. The company, says John Lopinto, manager/technology development, wants to create a data base that will provide a "consistent display" to viewers, avoiding the "hodgepodge of style and content" that results when many information providers put information into a data base.

Time will supply almost all information for the test; local information providers will be given up to 20% of the system's capacity. Another 20% of the teletext magazine will be ads or software that can be downloaded to a subscriber's home terminal. Time hopes to enlist local newspapers as partners when the service goes into commercial operation beyond the initial test sites. Sample frames shown in June 1982 included news, sports, maps, theater reviews and excerpts from books published by Time-Life Books. The data base will be updated on an hourly basis.

Administration of the Test

During the test Time officials hope to determine user perceptions of the value of a teletext service; what the usage might be; the possible effect of the service on other media; and how the company can work in partnership with local newspapers and cable systems to offer the service. Commercial rollout would not come before the next several years, McCarthy said.

Time Video Information Services vice president, Larry Pfister, said in June 1982 that users will probably be charged from $5 to $10 per month for the service, and that ad revenue—rather than subscription fees—would supply the bulk of the revenue. Time is creating an advisory council of advertising agencies and clients who will participate in the San Diego and Orlando tests.

Time has asked major equipment manufacturers to come up with PLP-compatible set top teletext decoders that would sell for $150 and have memory capacity of 64K. The preliminary RFP asked for specifications involving production of "hundreds of thousands" of the decoders.

Pfister said the use of a full video channel rather than just the vertical blanking interval would yield a larger and more marketable data base and could simulate interactive systems. Two-way systems require major increases in computer power as new users are added.

Although Time ran the test from late 1982 until late 1983, it was unable to devise a commercial teletext service that made sense. Two main problems seemed to be inability of manufacturers like Matsushita Electric Industrial Company to come up with inexpensive decoders, and the competition for consumers' time and money from other electronic media.

In November 1983, Time disbanded its teletext project, eliminating some 100 jobs. The project had reportedly cost between $15 million and $25 million. The company said it would maintain a small group to continue to study opportunities in electronic information services.

TIMES MIRROR CO.
Times Mirror Sq.
Los Angeles, CA 90053

Times Mirror Co. is a vertically and horizontally integrated publisher with major investments in printed and electronically delivered information services for businesses and consumers. The company's participation in electronically delivered services in 1977 consisted of two conventional TV stations and a few cable TV systems. But in 1978 it embarked on a major expansion into new delivery technologies. The company acquired a major cable TV company, Communications Properties, Inc., in 1978 for $129 million, more than tripling its cable TV customer count. It also invested $82.4 million to buy five television stations.

California Field Test

Early in 1981 the company formally announced a major videotext experiment using both cable television and telephone lines as delivery conduits, although in a published interview just before the test started, Times Mirror president Robert Erburu insisted that talk of a U.S. videotext market was premature.

Announcement of the test in February 1981 designated Telidon Videotex Systems Inc. as the turnkey builder of its $1 million plus system. Mission Viejo and Palos Verdes, both near Los Angeles, were selected as test sites, partly because of their proximity to Times Mirror cable TV headquarters and the *Los Angeles Times*, a major contributor of information to the service. Testing of the new videotext system involving 350 homes, a data base of more than 20,000 frames of information and more than 50 IPs began in mid-March 1982. Original announcement of the test said 200 homes would be involved, but the sample was expanded at the request of Bank of America, which agreed to fund incremental costs. Of the test homes, 150 were connected to Times Mirror's Mission Viejo cable TV system; the remainder on the nearby Palos Verde peninsula, were connected to the data base by telephone lines.

Test Results and Implications

In mid-1982 Times Mirror videotext executive James Holly said that daily usage of the system averaged 21.8 minutes per household according to early test results, with 1.4 people per home using the system on any given day. Holly said that 36.4% of all frames requested by users were archival in nature; 34.9% were index pages; 15.6% timely, such as news, and 3.1% advertising. Users requested 45.2 frames per session and viewed an average of 2.1 frames per minute. Usage of the 33,000 frame data base tended to spurt on weekdays after school hours because of extensive use by children playing video games on the system.

Initial results of the test have convinced Times Mirror officials of the importance of news, graphics and transaction capabilities to the service. "We're selling thousands of dollars worth of tickets [using the videotext system]," Holly said. Times Mirror hadn't committed itself to a commercial rollout of the service by mid-1982, but Holly noted that the publishing-broadcasting-cable company is "pretty heavily committed financially" to the videotext business. "We think this is a business that's here to stay."

The question of how to transmit videotext—by telephone or cable TV —in the early stages is apparently being answered in favor of telephone delivery. Although response times are about the same according to Holly, cable system delivery has been less reliable. He also said that as the number of users increases, the company is building more capacity to handle simultaneous users without having to buy more machinery. The ultimate goal, Holly said, is to be able to sell a computer system by 1984 for $3 million that would handle 4000 simultaneous users.

Test homes were supplied with Canadian-made color TV monitors and alphanumeric keyboards. Holly acknowledged that telephone-connected homes would be unable to make or receive calls while using the videotext system unless they acquired a second phone line, a fact which could make the service less popular. But test homes were screened carefully to eliminate those unlikely to use the service.

Times Mirror would not charge users initially for the service, but will ask them to pay during the final two months of the test. Usage fees had not been determined.

Comp-U-Star home shopping service, electronic yellow pages and electronic mail were among the communications and transaction services offered along with adaptations of Times Mirror publications such as the *Los Angeles Times* and *Popular Science* magazine. Other information and service providers included Bank of America, Ticketron, Sears Roebuck & Co., Waldenbooks and World Book, Inc.

Shortly before the test started Times Mirror agreed to form a joint venture with Infomart (Telidon's Canadian marketing company comprised of two of Canada's publishing companies), to develop, market and operate Telidon videotext systems in the U.S. with the first undertaking, the Times Mirror test. Videotex America planned to join local partners in other American cities to set up additional videotext systems. In mid-1982, Videotex America announced its first agreement with Phoenix Newspapers, Inc., publisher of *The Arizona Republic*, to explore consumer and commercial videotext opportunities in the Phoenix area. The agreement will give the publisher access to the results of the Times Mirror videotext test.

NOTES

1. "Revenues Up 30% for Top Electronic Data Publishers," *Information and Data Base Publishing Report* 2 (February 19, 1982): 1, 6.

2. U.S., Federal Communications Commission, *Notice of Proposed Rule Making*, p. 1, FCC Broadcast Docket No. 81-741, adopted October 22, 1981.

3. Ibid., p. 6.

4. William Broad, "Upstart Television: Postponing a Threat," *Science* 210 (November 7, 1980): 611-615.

Table 4.1: Videotext Tests and Commercial Services

Service or Host (Owner)	Location	Start Date	Transmission Medium	Receive[1] Sites	Display[2] Format
Consumer Services: Teletext (One-Way)					
KSL-TV (Bonneville International Corp.)	Salt Lake City, UT	6/78	broadcast TV	12	CEEFAX (20 lines of 32 characters)
KMOX-TV (CBS, Inc.)	St. Louis, MO	3/79	broadcast TV	NA	CEEFAX and Antiope
WKID-TV (Oak Industries)	Hollywood, FL	12/80	broadcast TV	250	16x32
WFLD-TV (Field Enterprises)	Chicago, IL	4/81	broadcast TV	50	CEEFAX
KNXT-TV (CBS, Inc.)	Los Angeles, CA	4/81	broadcast TV	100	Antiope
KCET-TV (Community TV of Southern California)					
Danbury News-Times (Dow Jones & Co.)	Danbury, CT	6/81	cable TV	150-200	Antiope
WETA-TV (Public Broadcasting System)	Washington, DC	6/81	broadcast TV	50	Telidon
KPIX-TV (Westinghouse Electric Corp.)	San Francisco, CA	10/81	broadcast TV	30	Antiope
KNBC (RCA)	Los Angeles, CA	10/81	broadcast TV	100	Antiope
KIRO-TV (Bonneville International Corp.)	Seattle, WA	4/82	broadcast TV	NA	CEEFAX
San Francisco State University	San Francisco, CA	4/82	cable TV	62,000*	NA
WKRC-TV (Taft Broadcasting)	Cincinnati, OH	8/82	broadcast TV	40	CEEFAX
WGBH (WGBH Educational Foundation)	Boston, MA	8/82	broadcast TV	20	Antiope

Table 4.1: Videotext Tests and Commercial Services (continued)

Service or Host (Owner)	Location	Start Date	Transmission Medium	Receive[1] Sites	Display[2] Format
Louisville Courier-Journal	Louisville, KY	8/82	cable TV and broadcast TV	NA 35	Antiope
Time Inc.	San Diego, CA Orlando, FL	10/82	satellite to cable TV systems	400	Telidon
Consumer Services: Viewdata (Two-Way)					
CompuServe Information Service (H&R Block)	Columbus, OH	1979	telephone	28,000	alphanumeric
Source Telecomputing Corp. (Reader's Digest Association)	McLean, VA	1979	telephone	20,000	alphanumeric
Electronic Information Service (AT&T)	Albany, NY	8/79	telephone	85	NA
Viewtron (Knight-Ridder Newspapers and AT&T)	Coral Gables, FL	7/80	telephone	160	modified CEEFAX
Channel 2000 (OCLC, Inc., and Banc One Corp.)	Columbus, OH	10/80	telephone	200	NA
Indax (Cox Communications)	San Diego, CA Omaha, NB	4/81	cable TV	200	16x32
BISON (Belo Corp.)	Dallas, TX	7/81	telephone	200	24x40
FirstHand (First Bank Systems, Inc.)	Minneapolis-St. Paul, MN	12/81	telephone	250	Antiope
Advertiser-Tribune	Tiffin, OH	2/82	telephone	NA	16x32
Times Mirror Co. and Infomart	Mission Viejo, Palos Verdes, CA	3/82	telephone and cable TV	350	Telidon
Star TEXT (Tandy Corp. & Capital Cities)	Tarrant County, TX	4/82	telephone	NA	16x32

Electronic Editions (Cowles Publishing Co.)	Spokane, WA	6/82	telephone	100	alphanumeric
Venture One (CBS, Inc.)	Ridgewood, NJ	9/82	telephone	200	PLP[3]
HVC Corp.	Dallas, TX	10/82	telephone	—	alphanumeric
ConTelVision (Continental Telecom)	Manassas, VA	late 1982	telephone	—	Antiope
Keycom (Centel Corp., Field Enterprises, Honeywell, Inc.)	Chicago, IL	mid-1983	telephone	—	PLP
Business Services: Viewdata (Two-Way)[4]					
Dialog Information Services (Lockheed Corp.)	Palo Alto, CA	1972	telephone	15,500	alphanumeric
Dow Jones News/Retrieval (Dow Jones & Co. Inc.)	Princeton, NJ	1973	telephone and cable TV	47,000	alphanumeric
SDC Search Service (Burroughs Corp.)	Santa Monica, CA	1/73	telephone	6500	alphanumeric
New York Times Information Bank (New York Times Co.)	Parsippany, NJ	1973	telephone	NA	alphanumeric
Agnet (State of Nebraska)	Lincoln, NB	1975	telephone	2400	alphanumeric
Project Green Thumb (U.S. Dept. of Agriculture)	Kentucky	1979	telephone	200	16x32
IN/FORM (Knight-Ridder Newspapers)	Philadelphia, PA	1/82	telephone	60	alphanumeric

[1] As of mid-1982.

[2] Alphanumeric services consist almost exclusively of letters and numbers, and occasionally include charts or primitive graphics. Displays range up to 80 characters per line but are dependent on the type of display device the customer uses.

[3] Presentation Level Protocol.

[4] Business services, actually more numerous than consumer services, are generally alphanumeric and higher-priced than consumer videotext services.

*Cable subscribers need touch tone telephones to communicate with the computer at San Francisco State University.

5

Viewdata in the United Kingdom: Prestel and Beyond*

by Peter Sommer

When long-heralded technological miracles finally arrive, reactions can be somewhat mixed: while the majority of the population is inclined to disbelief, some complain because the event is not miraculous enough.

So it has been with Prestel, the world's first full public viewdata service. The miracle it delivers, in the long term, is the possibility of a computerized information bank in every home. In the shorter run it brings a series of low cost information services to small businesses and professional practices, big business having enjoyed such facilities for some time.

INTRODUCTION

Prestel ceased to be a mere trial or demonstration in September 1979. By the end of 1980 it was available at local call rates to 62% of the telephone-owning population of the United Kingdom (the rest had to make long distance calls). Since July 1981, overseas customers have been admitted to the service, but at a fairly expensive basic call rate.

Prestel's current computer network consists of six storage computers from which radiate out a number of multiplexed telecom lines to permit access from many locations. There are more than 200,000 frames of information from more than 180 principal sources and 600 subsidiary sources. Shortly to be implemented across the network is the ability of one Prestel user to send messages to another—electronic mail—and by the end

---

*In this chapter, the British term *viewdata* is used as the generic term equivalent to *videotext*, used throughout the rest of the book.

of 1982, the "gateway" facility will allow Prestel users to access suitably designated computers owned by third parties (e.g., banks, travel companies and mail order houses) to confirm bookings and orders and to allow home/office banking transactions. Both these facilities have been in large-scale experimental operation since March 1982.

Prestel thus brings to reality some of the predictions made in the last 10 to 15 years. And yet the story is far from being a complete success: for a start, the familiar predictions have been fulfilled in ways which are subtly different from most people's expectations. Second, it is now generally agreed that Prestel's sponsor, the British Post Office (BPO), now renamed British Telecom (BT), mismanaged the promotion and marketing of their new service. By the end of 1980, they were saying in mid-1979, there would be at least 100,000 users and growth would be exponential thereafter. However, at the end of 1980 there were less than 10,000 registered sets and by June 1982 there were 16,350. Prestel has had one of the slowest rates of growth of any new technological medium.

So the Prestel community and its observers asked the question: did too few people know how useful Prestel could be, or was Prestel not offering what was needed? The answer to that question requires the understanding that technological miracles always seem to arrive in slightly different forms from those described by the futurists—and never have quite the predicted effects. To make life more difficult for analysts, Prestel has developed a rich variety of add-ons and look-alikes, not all of which benefit Prestel as a commercial operation.

It is inevitable that, as other national systems approach live public service status and as North America plans its own systems, the British experience be examined in detail to determine reasons for success and failure. The extent to which other countries have latched on to the technology, and the speed with which large mainframe computer manufacturers have rushed to produce add-on packages for "private viewdata," are phenomena not to be overlooked. However inept Prestel's earliest efforts may now seem in retrospect, the main thrust of our analysis should be to show the unique circumstances in which Prestel was conceived and the painful process, far from over, of discovering exactly what viewdata is.

HISTORY OF PRESTEL

Prestel illustrates the "accidental" theory of history; promoted as a means of extending the use of the telephone network during non-peak hours, it began its life by being used at the busiest times. It was announced as a service of instant appeal in the home, but it is doubtful that many ordinary residences will have a Prestel set before 1983. With the benefit of hindsight it is easy to spot the wrong decisions, but a more charitable view is that most of the mistakes were both necessary and enlightening.

Fedida's Concept

Sam Fedida, an engineer working on user friendly computer systems, joined the BPO in 1970. Combining his interest in easy-to-use computers, the Post Office Research Department's interest in television, and the Post Office's desire to maximize non-peak usage of telephone lines, Fedida proposed an information retrieval system that could be relayed over the ordinary public switched telephone network and displayed on an adapted domestic television set. By 1974, a group of enthusiastic engineers had produced a working model: the essence of viewdata composed of a one color display, upper case letters only and no graphics.

The then director of telecommunications, Sir Edward Fennessey, backed the idea and decided to bring the service to commercial reality. The following criteria were laid down:

1. The system must be reliable. Frequent breakdowns would cause it to be discredited.

2. It must be simple enough for anyone to use without instruction.

3. It must be fast and enable as many people as possible to access the service simultaneously.

4. The costs of both sets and computer centers must be as minimal as possible.

5. A network of computers storing identical data—rather than an interconnected network of different data bases—was to be established.

Other important decisions followed. Britain's television authorities had been, during the same period, developing teletext, which began full service in November 1976. The teletext industry had agreed to certain standards for display and BPO viewdata (it was not yet called Prestel) decided to adopt the same. (This had the advantage for the set manufacturers in that one character generator and display device would work both for broadcast teletext and the new viewdata service.) Early in 1981 this decision was further solidified and both CEEFAX/ORACLE and Prestel agreed to keep in step in terms of display system enhancements. The BPO also decided to relax its hitherto unbending monopoly on the supply of devices attached to the public network, permitting viewdata set manufacturers to incorporate their own modems.

Launching of Prestel

Regarding content, the BPO decided that its most appropriate role was as a "common carrier"—i.e., so long as no laws were broken (e.g., those relating to defamation, blasphemy or pornography), no editorial control would be exercised. Anyone who could pay would be allowed to become an information provider.

The name Prestel was chosen when it was discovered that the word "viewdata" could not be made proprietary. A team headed by a former Cambridge architect, Alex Reid, began to take shape. It was his task to set the aims and deadlines for the new service and spark public enthusiasm. The problem he faced—and it is one that Prestel still lives with—was how to give viability to a service designed for mass rather than specialized usage. In particular:

- How do you encourage set manufacturers to produce the large quantities that will make possible low prices for purchase or rental?

- How do you persuade potential information providers (IPs) to put up useful frames of information at the start-up of this service?

- How do you persuade the rest of the BPO to commit the necessary system resources when there is also a demand for improved exchanges, extended data communications facilities, fiber optic lines, satellites, microwave links, etc?

Reid's approach can be summarized by the following quotation: "If you are trying to achieve takeoff, it is foolish to do it at half throttle." A successful propagandist, Reid took Prestel through its test service, public trial service, and finally to its public launch in late 1979. In March 1980 he left and began working for the BPO in a higher-level position. Without Reid it is doubtful whether Prestel would have moved so rapidly from development to commercial service, but his lack of success in meeting his objectives has left Prestel with its current problems.

- He failed to get central government backing for the massive push required to establish Prestel as a public utility. Funding for Prestel came solely from within BPO resources. There were no promises of support for educational programs and only limited help for public information data bases.

- The TV industry reacted cautiously. The British Radio Equipment Manufacturer's Association (BREMA) kept looking to the government or to big IPs to take viewdata beyond the expensive prototype set stage. In part, they were discouraged to go for mass market production because of an early promise by the BPO, later withdrawn, to market a £50 adaptor. (Until the arrival of the £170 adaptor in late 1980, typical costs for "dedicated" viewdata TV sets were £900-£1200 for color and £600 for black and white. In the U.K. an ordinary color TV set costs approximately £275.)

- The IPs had a great deal to learn. No one had written electronic file cards before. The only people with experience were the handful of employees of CEEFAX and ORACLE, the broadcast teletext organizations, and the first data bases to appear were highly experimental. But as the test service became the public trial and then a public service, the IPs had to ask themselves hard questions. What was the point of providing quizzes, recipes or entertainment guides if the domestic users were not there? Given that any information source is only worthwhile if used, what was the financial justification for putting any detailed data on Prestel?

Change in Emphasis

When Reid left he was replaced by a former IP, Richard Hooper, who immediately announced a consolidation program. In effect BT still expects Prestel to be a domestic service, but for at least 1982 and 1983 it is concentrating on business applications. Going for a series of non-overlapping business markets means that IPs can target the data bases to those who can afford the sets at the present prices. As of mid-1982, Prestel marketing consists of sector product development managers and a small direct marketing sales force. Some IPs are skeptical of the latter approach. In the meantime, the set manufacturers have specific users for their equipment and they can obtain the volume required to enable them to offer mass-priced sets in two years' time. For the time being, the growth of Prestel will depend on the activities of IPs, aided by the increasing interest in private viewdata, which increases the set population by adopting the same set of technologies for company-wide information-sharing purposes. The implications of these decisions will be examined at the end of this chapter.

Richard Hooper defined his attitude by the following questions: Would you buy Prestel in order to get the weather forecast? No. Would you look at the weather forecast if it was on a Prestel set that you had bought for some reason central to your business? Yes.

PRESTEL, FROM THE USER'S POINT OF VIEW

Locating Information

From the user's point of view, viewdata is simplicity itself. When the user touches the "viewdata" or "Prestel" button on his control pad, the television picture is replaced by a display inviting him to key a number for service. Through the television speaker comes the sound of a phone off the hook. Following the directions on the screen, the user keys a single digit: this is an instruction to the viewdata set to dial into the local Prestel computer.

Once a connection to Prestel has been made, an announcement on the screen invites the user to put in his password. (In fact the terminal has already sent a multi-digit identifier to the Prestel computer as the first step in being recognized, but the user is unaware of this.) The user keys in his four-digit password and then, assuming the Prestel computer has recognized it, the screen clears again, this time to give a "welcome" message.

From now on, the user has the whole of the Prestel service at his command. He uses a keypad similar to that of a touch-tone phone, and all of his instructions are by means of single digits or combinations of *, # and digits. Any page on Prestel can be reached by keying a single stroke at a time and using a series of menus or indexes. Page 0 and those immediately following are provided as a free service by BT. All other pages are put up by the IPs, which is Prestel's name for publishers. Finally, if both BT and the IPs have done their jobs, the user should find himself at an "end frame" containing the information he was seeking.

Faster means of locating the end frame exist. Any page on Prestel can be accessed by keying *(the number of the desired page)#. Printed directories guide the user to the desired page.

Figure 5.1 shows how to locate information by single- or double-digit-keying from Page 0, which is always the first page seen. As an alternative for reaching the same page, an experienced Prestel user might have remembered, for example, that Viewtel had some information on what's on at the cinema on page 202193a and merely keyed *202193a #. Most regular users of individual Prestel pages seem to be able to remember rather long numbers and to key them "direct." ("Keyword access," i.e., using words via an alphanumeric keyboard, is not currently

Figure 5.1: Locating Information on Prestel

PRESTEL   0a   0p
PAGE 0
1 GENERAL INTEREST INFORMATION
2 BUSINESS INFORMATION
3 LOCAL INFORMATION
4 YOUR OWN INDEX
5 LIST OF TOPICS
6 LIST OF INFORMATION PROVIDERS
7 WHAT'S NEW ON PRESTEL
8 PRESTEL GAZETTE &
  PRESENTING PRESTEL
9 TALKING BACK

If you wanted to find out what's on at the cinema you could take either of the routes outlined below. Alternatively consult the section "Information on Prestel" to find the page number for cinemas and key it directly.

— Key 1 — — Key 5 —

PRESTEL   1a   0p
GENERAL INTEREST INFO.
1 NEWS & WEATHER
2 SPORT & HOBBIES
3 ENTERTAINMENT
4 HOLIDAYS, TRANSPORT, TRAVEL
5 MARKETPLACE
6 ADVICE
7 GOVERNMENT INFORMATION
8 EMPLOYMENT
9 BOOKS & REFERENCE
0 OTHER INFORMATION

PRESTEL   199a   0p
ALPHABETIC LIST OF TOPICS
11 A   18 H   24 O   30 U
12 B   19 I   25 P   31 V
13 C   20 J   26 Q   32 W
14 D   21 K   27 R   33 Y
15 E   22 L   28 S   33 Z
16 F   23 M   29 T
17 G   24 N

Key 3   Key 13

PRESTEL   13a   0p
ENTERTAINMENT
1 GAMES YOU CAN PLAY ON PRESTEL
2 WHAT'S ON
3 MUSIC
4 PLACES & BUILDINGS TO VISIT
5 STORIES
6 SPORTS & HOBBIES
7 RESTAURANTS & PUBS
8 FUN PAGE
9 HOROSCOPES

PRESTEL   1993a   0p
C · ALPHABETIC LIST OF TOPICS
11 Cal - Cap
12 Car
13 Cas - Cat
14 Ch - Ci
15 Ci
16 Coa - Col
17 Com
18 Con
19 Coo - Cov

Key 2   Key 14

PRESTEL   131a   0p
WHAT'S ON
1 CINEMAS
2 THEATRES
3 NIGHT LIFE
4 CONCERTS
5 OTHER EVENTS

PRESTEL   19934a   0p
Ch - Ci
13 CHARTERED SURVEYORS
14 CHARTER FLIGHTS
15 CHEMICAL INDUSTRY
16 CHILDREN'S PAGES
17 CHILDREN'S STORIES
20 CHILE
21 CHINA
22 CHRYSLER
23 CHURCHES
24 CINEMAS

Key 1   Key 24

PRESTEL   1311a   0p
CINEMAS
1 FAMILY LIVING
2 MERCURY 332
3 TIME OUT
4 VIEWTEL 202

Key 4

VIEWTEL 202 202193a   0p
WHATS ON
Cinemas
1 BIRMINGHAM (CITY CENTRE)
2 BIRMINGHAM (SUBURBS)
3 SOLIHULL
0 WHAT'S ON INDEX

— Key 1 —

VIEWTEL 202   2021931a   0p
BIRMINGHAM CINEMAS (CITY CENTRE)
ABC 1 BRISTOL ROAD
(CURRENT PROGRAMME DETAILS)
ABC 2
(CURRENT PROGRAMME DETAILS)
ABC 3
(CURRENT PROGRAMME DETAILS)
⊡ FOR MORE CITY CENTRE CINEMAS
9 CINEMAS INDEX   0 WHAT'S ON

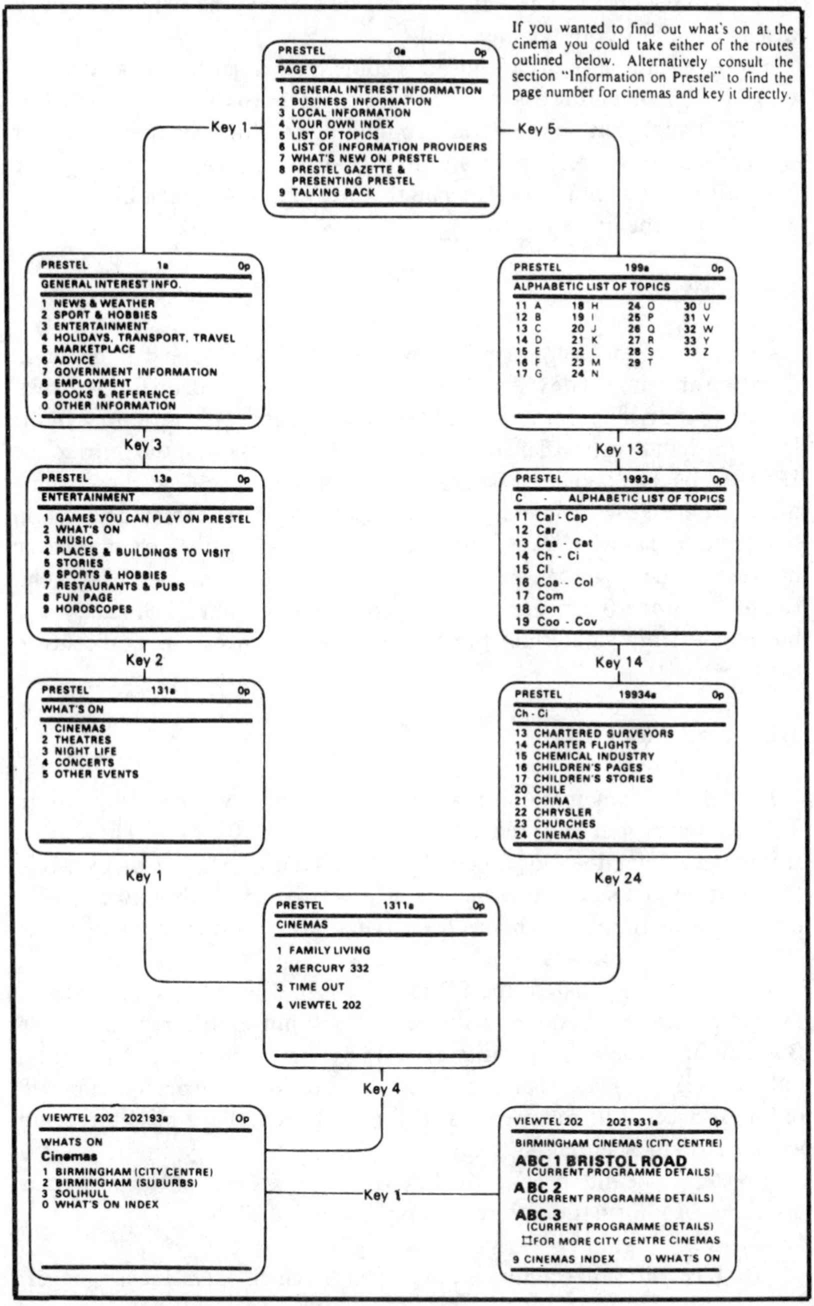

Source: Prestel. Reprinted with permission

possible on regular Prestel, though it will probably be used for searching indexes in the future. The technique can be used via the Prestel Gateway, discussed later in this chapter.)

Prestel's data base organization is sometimes described as a "decision tree," but the structure and choice of frames is up to the IP. The structure should be such that no user winds up looking at a frame without knowing where to go next—perhaps to another, related end frame, or perhaps to a new sub-index. One analyst has said that writing for Prestel is like starting a book with the index.

User Costs

The costs to the user are as follows: 1) a local telephone call, based on duration and time of day; 2) a Prestel computer charge, again time-related; and 3) an individual frame charge for those frames carrying a price in the top right-hand corner. The first two charges go to BT and the third to the IP, after BT has taken a 5% commission. Index frames and those which merely route a user from one place to another tend to be free; the decision to charge, and at what level, is up to each IP. The system allows any charge between 0.1 pence and 99 pence. Typical frames for residential usage tend to cost between 0.5 pence and 1.5 pence (about three U.S. cents) and business-oriented material from 1.5 pence to 10 pence (about 20 cents in the U.S.).

What Prestel Can Do

Prestel's fundamental unit is a frame of information. It can hold up to 960 characters, but in practice that means 80 to 110 words. The Prestel storage computer does not "understand" what is on the frame, or, except in the most limited sense, how one frame is related to another. Each frame can give the user up to 10 choices for his next frame. However, it is up to the IP to see the routes make sense to the user.

The neatest way to describe a Prestel frame is as an electronic file card. Prestel permits no keyword searching. It will not even carry out simple Boolean functions (e.g., identify answers by means of "yes/no" routines) unless the IP has made that a deliberate feature. To those brought up with online services, this represents a major limitation. They misunderstand what viewdata is supposed to do.

Prestel is meant to be a highly cost-effective solution to particular problems of information dispersal and collection. Thus:

- It requires no training in controlled thesauri, operating languages, or Boolean algebra, just the simple use of numbers on a pad. In the jargon, it is "user-friendly."

- It uses cheap terminals (a standalone adaptor containing control and display logic, modulator and modem is now £170 plus value added tax (VAT), and the price will fall).

- It uses the ordinary public switched telephone network.

- IPs can create data bases using journalists, not trained computer personnel.

- Information on Prestel can be rapidly updated. It will be available seconds after an IP has hit the final "end Edit" key.

- Viewdata permits users to send a pre-formatted message to any IP; and, with the aid of an alphanumeric keyboard, users can send messages to each other, though the process is presently semi-experimental.

The limitations of Prestel are undeniable, however:

- Both users and IPs are stuck with the "file card" mode of information display. Thus Prestel cannot readily be used for situations in which one line or one word responses are all that are required. By the same token, an answer that requires more than 110 words is awkward to handle and must send the user on to a series of "next" frames, which is tedious. It may be that computer technology will completely replace books, but it won't be viewdata that does it!

- Because there is no keyword searching, once a data base exceeds a certain size, the user must key through index after index without getting answers.

- If a data base has been poorly constructed, it may take the user a very long time just to find out that the desired information is not available.

- The service is never 100% available. Each Prestel retrieval computer has a limited number of ports. Just like any other part of the public telephone service, a retrieval computer can become congested.

- Prestel is not a live, instantly updated service. Thus if a user is watching a very volatile frame (e.g., stock market prices), once he has called it up from Prestel no alteration will appear on his screen even though the IP has sent an alteration to the computer. The user must keep summoning the frame anew if he thinks it might be changing.

Uses of Prestel

After a period of experimentation, Prestel's IPs have emerged with certain guidelines as to the strengths and weaknesses of the medium. Prestel can be used as:

- A first port of call in many information inquiries. As such it replaces both conventional reference books and periodicals. It also removes the burden from many services currently provided by conventional telephone. However, in a number of cases, the inquiry, having started out on Prestel, may continue using traditional techniques. Basic company statistics and media advertising are two obvious examples.

- A quick reference device where the linear form of printed material restricts the range of options open to the reader but where Prestel's multi-choice approach is more realistic. But the situation must not demand sophisticated keyword search, e.g., travel timetables, consumer information and public service announcements.

- A means of conveying rapidly changing information. With the caveat that Prestel is not truly real time, it can give significant advantages over any other medium available to the mass audience. Thus Prestel will not give the quality of service on stock exchange prices required by stockbrokers, but the private investor no longer has to wait for tomorrow's paper to see how his portfolio is progressing. Similarly, Prestel cannot give minute-by-minute accounts on how the seating plan in a particular airplane is being filled up by airline representatives across the world (though the airline's own computers can). It will give unrivaled information to travel agents and potential travelers on updated timetables and journey and holiday availabilities. (In early 1981 the travel trade was the single biggest user of Prestel.)

- A simple message handling service. In their present form response frames (user-to-IP) are used for further information requests, direct ordering and market research-type polling. Large international companies use it for inter-company communication because even now Prestel is cheaper than most other computer/ telecoms services.

- A form of advertisement. Unlike most advertising today, Prestel advertising cannot be based on the passivity of the user/target audience.

Advertising

Some IPs have experimented with including ads on information frames but the Prestel frame is too small to be treated like a newspaper page on which display advertising and editorial matter coexist. Other IPs have tried putting the word "Adflash" and a routing opportunity at the bottom of a frame in the hope that a user will follow it. This is rather like a commercial television station asking its viewers if they want the service with or without ads! Figure 5.2 shows a typical viewdata advertisement.

The most successful Prestel ads tend to be like earlier forms of advertising and concentrate on informational content—i.e., announcing the availability of particular goods and services. Thus Prestel is appropriate for classified advertising (its routing structure, if used creatively, can shorten the user's search time considerably) or for advising a potential customer of what specific goods or services best meet his needs. An ad can be withdrawn as soon as the item is sold.

Prestel can also be used for sponsored features which inform the user while promoting a particular range of services or goods. One of the data bases created by this writer, for example, uses a variation of this. LOTC is an IP that supplies prices on over-the-counter securities. On the grid giving each price is a Prestel route to a small data base about the company whose shares are being quoted. The company is eager to present its corporate image to the investment community and so is willing to pay to have its data base put up. As a result, LOTC can provide its current prices free to users (or free of frame charges anyway). This shows how Prestel can subtly alter the relationship between advertising and editorial.

These uses of Prestel reflect the present capabilities of the service. Many developments have been announced, together with dates for implementation. For these to be understood though, it is necessary to look in greater detail at its fundamental practices and technology. (For information on the technology of videotext in general see Chapter 2.)

Figure 5.2 Advertisements on the Prestel system provide viewers with instant information on the availability of goods and services. Courtesy Prestel.

Networking

An important aspect of viewdata technology which is largely invisible though absolutely essential is its networking capability, which is what transforms viewdata into a truly mass market vehicle. The facilities described earlier present little challenge to writers of conventional computer software, but there are two elements which make viewdata very different from anything that has preceded it. First is the large number of users—both consumers and IPs. A viewdata computer must be able to carry out a large number of transactions (i.e., displaying frames at once to a large quantity of consumers, accepting many simultaneous "updates" of information and making them available instantly to as many users as necessary). Second, it must perform all of this on a nationwide (or even global) scale. In fact, most of the activity inside a viewdata retrieval computer is concerned with networking and the compilation of accounts, not with the storage of information.

Viewdata technology thus consists of a series of trade-offs. Too many descriptions of home information retrieval services have not troubled themselves with some essential questions: Can ordinary, untrained people use it? Will the economics work out so that they can afford it? How many people can use the service at the same time? Prestel represents one series of realistic answers.

As will be seen later, a great deal of Prestel is the result of the happenstance of particular individuals at particular times. The critical decisions about Prestel's commercial structure—and hence its social positioning—were made in the peculiar atmosphere of a publicly owned communications utility where the requirements of profitability, social responsibility, simultaneous independence from and reliance on central government and the desire to be technologically innovative dance complicated steps around each other.

THE COMMERCIAL BASIS OF PRESTEL

Prestel's commercial form is the result of a series of historical accidents of birth. (Public viewdata systems in several other countries resemble the British model, although the United States will see a different pattern.) Prestel is the invention of Britain's publicly owned telecommunications authority, or PTT. Until recently both the PTT and the postal service belonged to the same giant public corporation, the BPO. In mid-1980, the Conservative Government announced that it was splitting the postal and telecommunications services, the former remaining the Post Office, the latter becoming British Telecom (BT).

BT, like most PTTs worldwide, has had a monopoly on supplying communications links. Although it is shortly to lose some of its powers and parts of it may be sold off to private interests, its monopoly has been extended to the supply of all equipment that is attached to the system (including telephone instruments, exchanges and modems).

Prestel thus evolved as a three-way partnership among BT, set manufacturers and IPs.

- *BT* provides the telephone lines, switching and the system of Prestel retrieval and update computers. It charges fees for system usage. It began by claiming that it was acting as a common carrier. (The common carrier policy has now undergone some modification, which is discussed later in this chapter.)

- *The set manufacturers* provide the special viewdata TV sets or adaptors which enable customers to use an ordinary set. Their incentive is the sale of a piece of equipment and the possibility of being able to master the new technology being created in their own backyard and then storm world markets. (No such storming has in fact taken place.)

- *The IPs* are Prestel's publishers. It was recognized right from the beginning that Prestel would attract successful print publishers as well as IPs drawn from other fields.

IP Costs

For the IP in the U.K., the cost of entering the business has been, on the surface, modest. BT asked most of them for £4000 per annum as a registration fee plus £4 for each frame rented; in 1981, the figures were £5000 and £5, respectively. While IPs must incur the same costs of information gathering and editing as in print publishing, they have no printing or distribution costs. The only bit of equipment the IP needs is a special keyboard for entering information into the computer.

Since viewdata publishing seemed cheap, a number of organizations rushed into the business without thinking through what they were going to offer.

A cost breakdown supplied by one large IP is as follows:

Communications and Prestel charges	12%
Manpower	41%
Research and development and consultants' fees	11%
Office space and overhead	23%
Promotional	7%
Other	6%

(This particular IP has its original information from its parents more or less on tap and hence "free.")

As later chapters in this book show, the costs of being an IP in other countries vary. In Germany, for example, IPs may have to own storage computers; in Canada, the IP needs expensive editing equipment; and in the U.S., the IP may be the system owner incurring all the costs but garnering all the revenues.

There is no such thing as a "typical" IP operation any more than there is a "typical" book, magazine or newspaper publishing enterprise. One IP, Careerdata, succeeded with a population of only 25 sets—they were all in the offices of university appointments boards and the service undertook to update students about current opportunities. Another IP, Intercom Videotex, supplies relatively few frames, but these give rapidly updated details of commodity prices and are thus frequently accessed by their users. Other IPs cannot possibly succeed until the residential market arrives. Appendix 5A suggests the range of annual costs by examining three hypothetical IPs with different ambitions.

Number of IPs

The total number of main IPs has remained at approximately 140 since the early days of the trial service. (Of the 187 IPs on the system as of spring 1982, nearly 50 are international and do not offer services for domestic use.) But there has been a significant number of dropouts and replacements over the years. At least three of Britain's national newspapers were IPs at one stage, but never produced substantive data bases. Provincial newspaper groups are well represented, notably the *Birmingham Post* owners of Viewtel, an electronic newspaper.

The variety of information available on Viewtel is shown on the index frame in Figure 5.3. Two attempts at providing sports results have failed— Sportsdata and Extel Sport (both had strong financial backing, but the market didn't exist); and national organizations like the Confederation of British Industries (CBI) ceased to become main IPs and used bureau services as well. One large national discount store, Comet Warehouses, withdrew after a few years when it decided that its customers were not users of Prestel. Already there is a rich repertoire of stories of success and failure—nearly all of them due to commercial wisdom or the lack of it.

Investment in Prestel

BT's financing of Prestel operates in commercial confidence. It regards Prestel as a separate profit center which produces its own accounts; BT

Figure 5.3 An index page from Viewtel, Britain's electronic newspaper, offers viewers a wide range of topics to choose from. Courtesy Prestel.

charges Prestel for the area it occupies in BT buildings, for its staff seconded to them, even for telephone calls. Expenditures through 1981 are believed to exceed £35 million. Now that it has achieved the first stage of public service, annual costs are believed to be around £16 million. Revenue in 1980 is thought to have been just over £2 million. The tariff structure is designed for mass market pricing, so to break even, about 200,000 customers must each spend £100 on the Prestel system per year. Since it has no prospect of reaching that figure in the near future, Prestel trimmed some costs in September 1981, shutting down eight computer centers and reducing overhead.

The investment by set manufacturers is similarly hard to assess. There are no great profit stories. The three suppliers of chip (integrated circuit) sets have been Mullard (part of the Dutch Philips group), Texas Instruments and General Instruments. Mullard now has a second generation chip set, colloquially called Lucy; Texas Instruments has dropped out and GI, the most recent entry, seems to have established itself well. No outsider knows the development costs.

A number of leading British TV set manufacturers have produced viewdata sets though so far all of them have been on limited runs and have relied in part on custom built rather than mass production lines. Philips, Pye, Thorn, GEC and STC have all persisted and produced several generations of models. In addition ITT has produced a particularly popular 16-inch model and Sony, which has manufacturing capacity in South Wales, has produced several sleek models.

Only one adaptor has come from a major TV set manufacturer—Pye (again part of Philips). The remainder have been developed by small purpose-created new companies associated with microcomputers, e.g., the Tantel, the Ayr, the Bee, the Ace and the Radofin.

The IPs are not only reticent about costs but have plenty of opportunities to hide them even from themselves. Few IPs are currently creating information sources solely for Prestel, but are adapting what they already have. Each IP has his own method of internal costing—as noted earlier, telecoms costs may be less than 12% of the total "real" cost. A crude estimate suggests that each frame on Prestel costs £50 to put up; in that event, IPs have invested £9 million. One of the largest IPs once said that his firm expected to spend £2 million before making a profit. Looking at the examples in Appendix 5A, it can be seen that fairly large quantities of frame accesses at a typical one pence charge must be made before profit is achieved. In practice a number of IPs do not seek direct profits from Prestel but use it as a means of making information about themselves available. The travel trade is a good example of this. In addition, many umbrella IPs operate on a fee basis, so that the losses are taken by their clients. When the total spent by all three parties in the Prestel partnership—BT, manufacturers and IPs—is added up, it may reach £75 to £80 million.

The Information Providers

Information providers are the heart of Prestel. In early 1982 there were about 187 IPs and an additional 400 sub-IPs.

Print Publishers

As might be expected, a number of IPs are traditional print publishers. The giant International Publishing Corporation has two principal data bases on Prestel, but neither of them really reflects the extent of the empire that fathered them. Specialist services in agriculture, business and computing are offered, but most of the rest seems to consist of a series of experiments. No national newspaper, except the *Financial Times*, is on Prestel.

The only main IP book publishers on Prestel at this time are Macmillan and Guinness Superlatives. Macmillan is conducting a series of in-house experiments without impressive actual visible output. The data base of Guinness Superlatives, publishers of the best-selling *Book of Records*, presumably awaits the residential user.

Link House is a magazine publishing group with one title that is a national institution and accounts for a great part of its profits—*Exchange and Mart*, which consists simply of classified advertising. LHC, its Prestel vehicle, is an umbrella (see below). The actual Prestel presence of *Exchange and Mart* is currently rather disappointing, though presumably, given the medium's editorial qualities, it could become extremely important.

Umbrella IPs

Significant among IPs not from a print publishing background is the computer bureau Baric, owned jointly by Barclays Bank and the British computer giant, ICL. Baric quickly showed other IPs an exciting range of techniques—quizzes created by the ingenious use of routing structures, carefully designed frames and inventive graphics. Baric was one of the pioneers of the "umbrella IP" concept, the IP who doesn't create much original material himself but sells frames and facilities to those who do want to provide information without setting up a full scale Prestel IP unit. There are currently about 400 sub-IPs, as they are called, and already a number of them have left their original benefactors for other umbrella IPs—or have decided to become full IPs themselves. The trouble with the umbrella concept is that, if taken too far, the overall data base consists of many mini data bases and lacks coherence.

One other great propagandist of the umbrella concept is Mills and Allen, a general purpose industrial group with particular interests in advertising. Its Prestel division had an enthusiastic managing director, Richard Hooper, who later became director of Prestel.

Another umbrella IP was founded by Malcolm Smith who left Prestel for private enterprise. He had invited the first set of IPs on to the system and then went on to set up AVS Intext, a company which helps IPs who find the Prestel going difficult. Its clients included the Confederation of British Industries, Classified Teledata (a telephone-based classified service) and Townsend Torsen, the cross-channel ferry service. But interestingly enough AVS Intext now sees its future more as a Prestel publisher— inventing new editorial concepts or forming joint ventures—than seeking clients.

Other IPs

Most of the other IPs are organizations who think that Prestel can help them in their existing businesses. Thus a number of airlines, travel companies, direct mail selling organizations, banks and credit card companies appear. Britain's well-regarded Consumer's Association has put a lot of effort into its data bases.

Much public service information, albeit selective, can be found on Prestel's frames. Many government departments issue copious announcements of their activities and services. Parliament, via the Central Office of Information, gives details of its bills and debts. Local services are listed by a special umbrella unit called Laser. A similar non-profit umbrella IP, the Council for Educational Technology, exists for universities, colleges and other educational institutions who either wish to announce their courses or carry out experiments into the educational value of Prestel.

Finally, there are a handful of companies that have come into being specifically to make their mark in viewdata. The interesting thing is that success in other fields seems to give little indication of likely success with viewdata. Sometimes the small new company, untroubled by a large hierarchy, is able to make the quick accurate judgments that are essential in any new enterprise.

The main IPs and their activities can be seen in Table 5.1, but the listing is deceptive, because it consists solely of those organizations who have a direct contractual relationship with BT.

Table 5.1: Prestel Information Providers

Category	Number
Umbrella services	12
Travel trade	25
Financial information	9
TV industry	5
Computer industry	9
Publishing—newspaper, magazine and book	29
Social information, education	9
Government	10
British Telecom	9
Advertising and marketing	2
International services	5
Banking, insurance, accounting	5
Agriculture	2
Medical, scientific	4
Broadcasting	2
Retail, mail order	3
Consultants	2
Legal	2
Recruitment	2
Classified ads	1
Bookmakers	1
Building, construction, property	3

Source: Compiled by the author. Categories exclude approximately 30 organizations that are largely international rather than domestic in their aims, as well as those that use Prestel as an inter-company device rather than as a medium for publishing information. No distinction is made between those IPs with less than 100 "live" frames and those with an excess of 10,000. Some IPs in this list may have their entire data base managed for them by one of the large umbrella service bureaus. Further, some substantial data bases may not appear in the list because they only have sub-IP status—two of Britain's big clearing banks, Dow Jones and the financial and credit agency Dun & Bradstreet fall into this latter position.

Prestel Customers

What the IPs, set manufacturers and BT itself want to know is: Who are Prestel's customers?

Large sums of money have been spent on market research but have failed to come up with useable answers. The Prestel system software allows an IP and BT to monitor the number of times in a given period that a particular frame has been accessed—but not by whom, and for what reason. A lot of current Prestel activity—on a population of 16,000 sets—is demonstration in showrooms, seminars and by owners. The same types of material keep reappearing—a news service, a game, a quiz, a message, an opportunity to order wine or theater tickets. Small wonder that these particular frames show exceptionally heavy traffic figures, but no one believes that such frames are typical of what Prestel will become in a few years.

Without exception the many questionnaires sent out have failed to come up with useful conclusions. In fact, given the way in which Prestel has developed as a series of non-overlapping services, no general conclusions can be drawn. A metal merchant may spend only five minutes a day looking at the few pages of commodity prices, but feel well satisfied with his investment in the medium, because the alternative—several calls to a London-based metal broker—would have been much more costly. A travel agent may look at Prestel briefly every half hour to check a holiday availability. A lawyer might use Prestel intensively for an hour and a half to check recent changes in the law on one day and then neglect his set for two weeks. An international sales manager might flip semi-regularly through the Prestel version of the *Wall Street Journal* (see Figure 5.4); check news from Fintel (the *Financial Times*) and *The Economist*; his assistant may use the travel pages regularly—and also perhaps the weather forecast. An associate might follow exchange rate movements. And they could all share one Prestel set.

So, no general conclusions can be drawn. Wise information providers ask themselves about the users of their services—no more.

PRESTEL TECHNOLOGY AND FUTURE ENHANCEMENTS

Storage Capacity

The Prestel network currently consists of eight large minicomputers or retrieval centers scattered throughout the U.K. and one more in Boston, MA, all holding identical data bases and linked by a direct wire to an update center in which the IPs input their frames. The minicomputers are GEC4080s with software written in Babbage and Coral; in mid-1981 they offered approximately 2000 ports (i.e., 2000 people country-wide could log on simultaneously).

The current Prestel network is configured like a star, presenting a number of limitations on the system's growth. First, Prestel's storage capacity can only be increased by enlarging the memory at each and every one of the

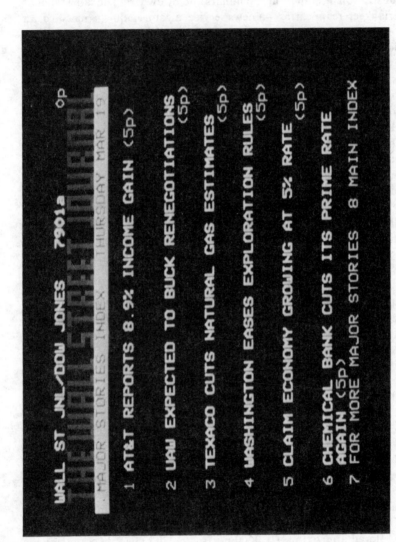

Figure 5.4 Information from Dow Jones and the *Wall Street Journal* makes Prestel a useful system for businesses. Courtesy Prestel

retrieval computers. Second, users can only access computers close to their homes or offices. This rules out the ability to send messages to users in other areas. BT has been working on improving the networking capabilities of the service under the name PANDA (Prestel Advanced Network Development Architecture). The new structure envisions an end to maintaining simultaneous data bases, but more sophisticated inter-computer links.

Prestel Graphics

Prestel display is a topic of much interest internationally. As noted earlier, the fundamental unit of storage and display is the Prestel frame. It consists of 40 characters across arranged in 24 lines. Two lines are used for system purposes, another two (minimum) for routing instructions from the IP to the user, leaving a realistic capacity of 80 to 110 words. Prestel uses seven colors, can create background color, offers double-height letters and has crude graphics. (The graphic block is a 3 x 2-inch shape and diagonals or curves can only be suggested rather than achieved.) There are also two curious gimmicks—a "flash" device which turns on and off, and a conceal/reveal arrangement, useful for quizzes, whereby certain parts of the Prestel frame remain blank until a "reveal" button is hit.

Prestel's transmission rate to the user is 1200 baud (bits per second), the highest speed that can with safety be sent over the public telephone network. The user responds to Prestel at the slower rate of 75 baud. A Prestel frame thus takes about six seconds to appear on the screen—fast enough for casual and domestic use. Higher speeds will only be possible with a vastly improved overall telephone network. If Prestel were to use a higher standard of graphics, it would take longer to transmit the frame; in addition the TV set would require a larger memory in order to fix the frame for display. These arguments persuaded BT not to attempt to emulate the Canadian service, Telidon, which has superior graphics capabilities.

Prestel uses a "serial attribute" means of transmission which means that in order for the display to change color, switch from letters to graphics, go from single-height to double-height, etc., a "control character" is required which occupies a space on the screen. Nevertheless, by means of careful design, attractive and varied frames can be created. (See Chapter 2 for a discussion of the differences in graphics among Prestel, Telidon and other systems.)

BT has demonstrated enhancements to the graphics capability of Prestel though none of them will be introduced before 1986. The first consists of Dynamically Redefinable Character Sets (DRCS), whereby a memory chip receives a series of instructions constituting a temporary replacement character set. Once this new character generator is in memory, frames can carry definite geometric shapes, maps, diagrams or non-Roman alphabets.

More exciting still is Picture Prestel, whereby full color, high definition pictures can be transmitted. Because of the time that would be required to transmit a color picture occupying a full frame, BT engineers suggest that only one-ninth of the frame be filled with high resolution pictures, leaving the rest for ordinary text and graphics.

Experimental pages currently up on Prestel feature Picture Prestel and the North American-type alphageometric graphics. Neither of these features is likely to be introduced until planned improvements in Britain's overall telecommunications exchanges and lines have been carried out in 1983.

Gateway

Trials have started to allow private viewdata systems to be accessed via the public system. The technology, known as "gateway," is also in use on the German service, Bildschirmtext. (See Chapter 9.) Then the information has to be retransformed and sent back into the Prestel computer and from there to the user.

The advantage of these complicated processes is that the system can yield enormous benefits once it is set up. Usually a remote computer can only be called up long distance or via a sophisticated and expensive terminal. Prestel provides affordable networking capability and inexpensive terminals. It is when one looks at the applications, however, that the extent of the revolutionary implications become clear:

- Until gateway, viewdata's ability to respond was very limited; it was the equivalent of sending a letter and not knowing whether it had been received. By taking the user into the computer of an IP, Prestel can deliver an instant response—e.g., a confirmed booking of a holiday or theater ticket, a confirmed order from a discount house (the mail order house can simultaneously check the credit of the customer), and even a banking transaction. Some of these gateway applications have already been tried in Germany.

- Until gateway, in order to put valuable information stored in other computers on Prestel, a lengthy process of creating Prestel frames and then storing them on a Prestel computer was required. Now gateway techniques can be used to format an information frame on Prestel simply on the demand of a customer. This lowers the IP's costs enormously. We can expect to see online-type services appearing initially probably on financial topics, and eventually as versions of reference books.

Prestel's first gateway applications started in spring 1982, on one computer. It may bring new organizations into Prestel, such as a bank or retail store concerned about escalating rents. If such powerful organizations believe they can reach people at home via Prestel, they will cheerfully trade off expensive rent costs in order to do so.

Private Viewdata

Parallel with the growth of Prestel has been computers using viewdata-like software as a means of data storage and retrieval. The principal applications have been:

- as an in-house information system—to replace internal memos and reports. It is possible to interface a viewdata system to a company's existing mainframe. Only internal telephone connections are needed but the private viewdata system has the twin advantages of ease of use and low cost terminals.

- as a means of communicating with retail outlets, e.g., mail order companies with home agents, car manufacturers with spare parts dealers, wholesale warehouses with retail stores, etc. From the user's point of view, the same terminal can access Prestel as well as the private system.

- as a means of selling information to a common interest group. The best live example of this is TOPIC, a service of the London Stock Exchange to member firms. Unlike Prestel, TOPIC operates in real time and offers a quality of service not possible on the public system. TOPIC is expensive compared to Prestel but cheap and effective in relation to more traditional online techniques.

Private viewdata software has been written not only for the GEC4080 but also for IBM, Honeywell, ICL and the DEC PDP 11 family. An annual budget for a 50,000 frame system with 16 ports used over the telephone system (16 ports merely specifies the number of simultaneous users, not the total number) would be, in 1981 prices, about £45,000, the same order of expense as for a medium-sized minicomputer system with general purpose commercial multi-tasking software.

Private viewdata has been slower in taking off than some of its advocates would like. TOPIC is a shining example. One reason for this has been Prestel's facility called the Closed User Group (CUG), which permits an IP to define the audience allowed to access his pages. This device has been used in a number of applications where private viewdata might be thought to have worked. One is a legal update service for solicitors and another is owned by a food giant to advise its customers. However, as prices of private viewdata systems fall, the economics of running CUGs on the public service may make less sense.

BT's provisions for third party data bases by means of the gateway software may persuade more companies to start storing their in-house data in viewdata format, just in case they want to transmit it or have it accessed via the public system. Software packages exist which speed up the process of reformatting conventional computer files into viewdata frames.

Private viewdata systems are also used by Prestel IPs as a means of storing their data bases offline and bulk updating new material to the Prestel Update Computer. One widely used configuration, the TM-3, is based on the DEC PDP11 family and even its smallest form is a complete viewdata system, albeit one only able to maintain a few hundred frames on a floppy disc at a time. However, by incorporating powerful word processing edit functions and sophisticated files of frames it can speed up the frame creation and modification process considerably.

Prestel and the Personal Computer

The personal microcomputers made by Apple, Commodore and now IBM may be a new means of accessing Prestel. Apple and Pet (made by Commodore) offer adaptors that will communicate with Prestel, and other manufacturers will follow. The display device is then not a domestic TV, but the microcomputer's video display unit (VDU).

Still another link between Prestel and a personal computer is to set aside certain Prestel frames in order to send computer programs into the memory of a micro that can be transmitted over telephone lines, a process called telesoftware. This is technically possible, but because of Prestel's relatively slow transmission time of six seconds per frame, only short programs can be readily accommodated.

Telesoftware

In the U.K. a number of attempts have been made to interface between Prestel and the home computer. The frame storage characteristic of viewdata slows things down but if a series of frames containing lines of computer instruction are sent in sequence, a home computer can receive a program almost as easily as if it was down-loading from cassette or disc. (Special arrangements have to be made to trap errors before they are put into the computer's memory store and, at six seconds a frame, Prestel is slow. Only short programs can be sent with ease.) One computer hobbyist magazine is offering telesoftware of a simple sort and experimental telesoftware is also offered from time to time by the teletext broadcasting authorities.

The Apple, Acorn, IBM, Pet and BBC microcomputers have approved adaptors to receive Prestel, and other popular machines are likely to follow. Microcomputers can be used to call up desired frames from Prestel on a regular basis, extract desired information from them, and then input data to locally created analytic programs, e.g., to chart the progress of commodity prices over a period. The microcomputer interface to Prestel is also a means to a "back door" version of keyword search. Whereas ordinary Prestel only responds to numeric commands, the microcomputer can contain a directory of Prestel pages which the user operates by inputting words on the keyboard. The micro then searches through its directory for a match and transmits the page number to the Prestel retrieval computer which in turn sends the desired page down the line.

The trouble with telesoftware is not only its technical achievement but also the need to identify situations in which it will be useful. Short programs tend to be simple and limited. What are the situations in which a user is so impatient to run a program that he can't wait for a more reliable cassette or diskette version? It may be that telesoftware has only a limited range of applications: for hobbyists, perhaps, or as updates to existing programs that have been acquired in more conventional forms. For example, a general purpose tax calculator could receive new data after tax changes have been announced.

For the person who is not a computer hobbyist (where the technical problems of program writing take precedence over the actual functioning of that program), it seems likely that processing power via Prestel will be done via the gateway, in a computer belonging to an IP.

In the U.S. the home computer could be very important. During 1980 two information services, accessible by using a home computer (e.g., Apple, TRS-80, Pet) as a terminal, began campaigning for customers in earnest. They were The Source, now owned by Reader's Digest, and Micronet, owned by CompuServe and behind it H & R Block. (See Chapter 4.) The services utilize the nonbusiness-hour-capacities of large time-sharing computer service bureaus and offer a mix of information utilities (you can access UPI's electronic morgue), message passing and computing facility. How far these services will attempt to link in with viewdata technology is so far not known.

PRESTEL AND THE FUTURE

Prestel's current problem is one of misplaced expectations. BT, in retrospect, oversold the medium both to itself and to its customers. Although BT started out wanting to increase evening and weekend domestic usage of its telephone network, it found that it was actually increasing daytime business use. The user-friendly operating system was designed for the public, but the only people who could afford it at the beginning were businessmen. But big business in particular is not short of sophisticated information sources and the means of storing them on computer. Few of Britain's major companies could find much of use on Prestel's data base.

Prestel has to attain its immediate growth by treading a very narrow path. Through 1983, the concentration must be on small to medium businesses—those who can afford the system but do not have access to more sophisticated computer sources. BT's marketing plan issued in November 1980 makes this plain; most resources are to be marshalled behind IPs active in appropriate sectors, with both BT and the manufacturers offering incentives to IPs who bring users on to the system.

The key to Prestel's survival is the quality of the information; IPs who make money will be those who can offer customers information they haven't had before, or in a more useful form than before, or at a previously unknown speed. IPs who have merely reformatted their existing information resources into viewdata pages could be in for a rough time. One IP has said, "The product we have to offer is the information, not the vehicle."

However, if the narrow path is successfully navigated, at the end enough sets will have been sold to encourage manufacturers to set up mass production lines and BT's network of computers will have begun to break even. At that point the more prosperous domestic user will start to appear.

Statistics on Prestel use to date show what one might have suspected— the demonstration, games and quiz pages are most popular, because the most prevalent Prestel activity is showing off the service, not actually using it. Research results are similarly unreliable—the sample can only be drawn from the small number of existing users and they in turn are not typical of the population at large, in that they were willing to invest in Prestel at all in its early phase.

If BT, manufacturers and IPs all stay the course, at some point between 1983 and 1985 Prestel may have generated enough momentum to assume its primary residential role. It will have done so because of the quality of the services offered on it, the usefulness of the user-to-user message service and the synergy provided by the growth of private viewdata systems. But if this happens, few users will find it remarkable; the miracle will have taken place over such a period of time that, without realizing it, Prestel will have moved instantly from the scarcely-believable to the commonplace. Prestel users will not think of themselves as such any more than people today categorize themselves as users of televisions, telephones, newspapers or cars. It will simply be a means of obtaining certain sorts of information. And only when such habits are established will Prestel be in a position to assume certain activities now performed by traditional communications media, like providing classified advertising or a way for retailers or service companies to communicate directly with customers.

What started out as a service that would be largely run by BT has, within a few short years, changed beyond recognition. Indeed, Prestel is not one service but many, sharing little except certain display characteristics, the "user-friendly" quality and some communications networks and protocols. BT itself is on its third or fourth substantive revision of its marketing strategy. Variants and add-ons to the basic service increase every week. Some industries, IPs and their customers have been seeing real benefits since mid-1980.

BT will not close Prestel because the long-term benefits to telephone usage are obvious, but it may well further revise its targets. The future of the other parties depends on their commercial agility—they operate in gold rush town conditions and many stakes will have barren yields.

In the meantime, the number of Prestel-based variants will continue to increase. The imminent deregulation of cable TV in Britain, at present used in two million homes but restricted to transmission of the three or four off-air channels plus a highly-controlled experiment in subscription TV, could have both BT and private operators seeking to partially abandon the public telephone network in favor of the different tariff structures and cultural expectations of cable.

So the revolution is happening—and it is far more complex than any of the forecasters or early participants ever imagined.

Appendix 5A: Annual Costs Accrued by Hypothetical IPs*

IP One: small service company; in effect selling Prestel printing facilities to anyone who wants them

Prestel registration	£5,000
Frame rental @ 750 frames	3,750
Prestel equipment (outright)	1,500
Prestel editor/secretary	7,500
Management	12,000
Office overhead	10,000
Promotion	6,000
Other costs, including telecoms	5,000
Total	£50,750

---

*It should be understood that none of these IPs actually exists and that there is a notable lack of frankness in statements about the financial viability of being an information provider.

IP Two: specialist information; frequently updated

Prestel registration	£5,000
Frame rental @ 400 frames	2,000
Prestel equipment (outright)	10,000
Prestel editors (3)	24,000
Management	12,000
Secretary	6,000
Researchers, information collectors	12,000
Office overhead	15,000
Promotion	8,000
Other costs, including telecoms	12,000
Total	£106,000

IP Three: large umbrella IP with a variety of large clients to serve and also some independent publishing ventures

Prestel registration (3 different ones)	£15,000
Frame rental @ 10,000 frames	50,000
Prestel equipment (outright)	13,000
Prestel editors (4)	32,000
Management, marketing—salaries	36,000
Secretarial	12,000
Office overhead	20,000
Promotion, publicity	15,000
Research and development	12,000
Other costs, including telecoms	25,000
Total	£230,000

6

Teletext in the United Kingdom

by Colin McIntyre

Whatever the outcome of the current standards battle in the U.S., teletext remains a British "first." It was developed by British broadcasting engineers in the 1970s, and Britain was the first country in the world to start a full public teletext service in November 1976. In less than a decade, this new broadcasting medium moved from the drawing board in a research laboratory to nationwide availability.

While acceptance of sets was modest at the beginning, by the start of the 1980s the predicted sales curve had shot upward. One major television rental company no longer offered its customers sets without teletext; all its latest models had built-in decoders. A recent British Broadcasting Corporation (BBC) audience research survey found that well over 50% of those questioned knew about CEEFAX, and about one in five of these people expressed an interest in acquiring a set in the near future.

By the end of 1982, the British viewer had a choice of four separate and distinct teletext services—one on each network. Two of these are CEEFAX services provided by the BBC, and two others are from the commercial teletext company, ORACLE. The ORACLE services run on the main commercial television network, known as Independent Television (ITV), and on the new Channel Four network. In some parts of the country regional teletext sections are input locally on the ITV channel.

Most European countries adopted the U.K. standard, and by mid-1982 there were more than a million teletext sets in Europe. Five hundred thousand of these were in Britain, with the rest mainly in Austria, Holland, Sweden and West Germany. In terms of penetration, Austria has led the way with more than 125,000 teletext sets in a television population of two million, against Britain's 500,000 in the much larger population of twenty million television homes. The arithmetic of teletext's adoption in the U.K.

shows a pattern typical of other consumer electronics devices: halting, even discouraging acceptance in the first several years, followed by a steep increase in sales.

As of the end of 1979, there were barely 50,000 TV sets in all of Britain equipped to receive teletext. By the end of 1980, the number had more than doubled to 120,000, and despite a general recession the television manufacturers began to take teletext seriously.

A major promotion campaign in which the manufacturers, the broadcasters, and the government all played a part took place in October 1981, which was decreed National Teletext Month. Public awareness increased considerably during this campaign, as did sales. By the end of the year production and sales had exceeded the forecasts, and there were then some 300,000 sets in homes or public places (e.g., restaurants, hotels, libraries). Table 6.1 summarizes the growth of teletext in the U.K. from 1976 to 1983.

Table 6.1: Growth of Teletext in Britain, 1976-1983

Year	Number of Teletext Sets Manufactured	Total Number of Teletext Sets In Use (cumulative)
1976-1978	15,000	15,000
1979	35,000	50,000
1980	70,000	120,000
1981	180,000	300,000
1982	650,000	950,000
1983 (forecast)	650,000	1,600,000

Source: British Radio Equipment Manufacturers' Association (BREMA)
Note: Although BREMA represents all the major TV set makers in Britain it does not cover imported sets, nor most of the small adaptor makers.

Half the color TV sets in Britain are rented, and the prevailing pattern of teletext usage is to rent these sets as well. Rental now adds less than one pound per month to the price of a standard color set, and the differential for purchasing a teletext set outright is now well under £100. There are more than 25 different makes of TV sets with teletext in Britain.

HISTORY OF TELETEXT

CEEFAX was actually developed by the BBC as a system of closed captioning for the deaf and hard-of-hearing. In 1971, the BBC's then director of engineering, Sir James Redmond, asked his head of research, Peter Rainger, to find a way of adding subtitles or closed captions without disturbing the picture of the hearing audience. When Rainger and his team came up with the solution that was to become CEEFAX, they realized they had something that was much bigger than a simple captioning system. In fact, their technique of transmitting digital data in an unused portion of the television picture could be used to transmit messages to the entire television viewing audience—forever shattering the notion that TV must be only a way of conveying entertainment motion pictures and sound.

Teletext's advance—from its laboratory version and first test signals in 1972, to a two year pilot trial beginning in 1974, and its acceptance as a full public service at the end of that period—was swift and painless. The broadcasters argued successfully that teletext was a simple broadcasting development, merely making better use of the existing television signal. The Minister of State at the British Home Office, which supervises broadcasting, authorized the two year trial.

Subsequently, teletext came under scrutiny by Lord Annan's Committee on the Future of Broadcasting, and in a government White Paper. Both endorsed that first decision. Broadcast teletext thus became a legitimate service in November 1976, and its position was firmly established in 1981 in the BBC's newest charter and license.

The economics of teletext favored this rapid process. The BBC's total initial capital cost was about £250,000 or $500,000. The second generation system installed in 1979 cost about the same, while running costs are about £240,000 annually, basically the salaries of 20 journalists.

Teletext is on the air during all the hours of broadcasting. In the case of the BBC, this means some 17 or 18 hours a day. ORACLE follows a similar pattern on the main ITV network, with more limited service on Channel Four, which does not start until the afternoon. It is possible that the start of Breakfast Television in Britain in early 1983 may affect the start-up times of teletext, and perhaps teletext viewing habits as well.

Even though the current audience for teletext is only one in 40 homes, the BBC decided from the start to address itself to the whole television mass audience. It is meant to entertain as well as inform, and is aimed at a wide range of popular tastes. News headlines, sports results, cooking recipes, quizzes and games, stock market quotations and seat availability on popular airlines are some of the mainstays of this approach.

The BBC's view is that teletext was designed for broadcast by broadcasters. Almost every strength in broadcast teletext stems from treating it as an ordinary arm of broadcasting; almost every shortcoming results from trying to graft on to it attributes that are not broadcast-related.

Teletext is something halfway between radio and television. It could be seen as a kind of *printed radio* displayed on the ordinary home television screen. In fact, teletext in many ways is closer to radio than it is to its host signal in television: it uses words to describe its message, and to a great extent avoids any reliance on a picture or graphic drawing.

The great advantage of teletext, and one that its developers at the BBC were quick to realize, is its simplicity. Teletext requires no extra bandwidths, no extra transmitters, no extra channels. It hooks into and becomes part of the ordinary television picture, even if what is being transmitted at that moment is a simple test pattern.

THE TRANSMISSION SYSTEM

The first "live" CEEFAX pages were broadcast by means of a single visual display unit (VDU) producing punched tape, which was then fed by hand into a 30-page memory store. It was a laborious but effective system.

By early 1975, CEEFAX had acquired its first computerized system. An off-the-shelf Computer Automation Alpha LSI/2 from the U.S. came into service, programmed by the British software house Logica. Affectionately known as "Esmeralda," this system served hard and well for four years. A team of BBC engineers and Logica programmers then developed a second generation transmission system, christened "Selene" after the goddess of the moon. It consists of three Digital Equipment Corporation PDP 11/34 computers which provide advanced editorial facilities and the high reliability required for a full public service.

The first of the three PDP 11/34 units handles the input from up to 16 VDUs continuously. The VDUs and the computer communicate at 9600 bits per second, so that when an editor calls up or inserts a page, it takes less than a second. The remaining PDP 11/34 computers operate parallel output systems, in an arrangement designed to give excellent reliability. They provide a variety of options for assigning teletext magazines to television data lines, and can handle more than the four data lines per television channel that are in use at the moment. Both CEEFAX and ORACLE began using four lines instead of two in October 1981.

Each output system has a separate, BBC-designed clock receiver. To make the best use of the accuracy available, extra header rows are broadcast, to ensure that the teletext clock is accurate to plus or minus one-fiftieth of a second.

Every teletext page, of course, carries the date and a running digital clock, a much-used facility, and one that is not available on Prestel. Another key feature of this second generation input system is its large library. Two RKO6 interchangeable disc stores operating in parallel provide 14 million bytes of memory, equivalent to some 10,000 teletext pages. The keyboards in use in the CEEFAX newsroom are Aston TCG3 and VG Electronics 1062s. They allow a wide range of editing facilities independent of the main computers; each has its own independent memory of eight pages.

The new keyboards and computers make full use of the updated 1976 technical specification, which includes a number of facilities not incorporated into the first generation equipment or decoders. These include the use of double height letters, background color, separated graphics and the hold facility which allows a map designer to change from one color to another without leaving a gap for a control character.

No sooner was the new BBC/Logica-designed system installed in the BBC Television Centre than it was being sold, in a variety of shapes and sizes, to overseas broadcasters. Two overseas broadcasters who took advantage of this opportunity to buy a complete CEEFAX-style system were Osterreichischer Rundfunk (ORF) of Austria and a company that has now become Keycom Electronic Publishing in Chicago. Keycom —jointly owned by the Centel Corp., Honeywell Inc. and Field Enterprises —not only broadcasts its KEYFAX service of "demand teletext" on the same push-button call-up system used for U.K. teletext, but also broadcasts a special service called NITE OWL over WFLD-TV between midnight and 6 a.m. each night (see Figure 6.1). NITE OWL is a series of rotating pages that can be seen by all viewers whether they have decoders or not. Keycom is now offering its output of teletext by satellite to 19 million other viewers throughout the U.S.

In each case, ORF and Keycom have benefitted not only from the BBC's broadcasting teletext experience, but they have also been able to get Logica to provide enhancements to the existing system, giving them the very latest that is available in teletext. In Australia, Channel BTQ-7 in Brisbane has bought a similar system, with some extras for the Australian markets.

The Austrians have maintained a particularly close liaison with the work going on at the BBC, and at the time of writing have managed several firsts of their own, ranging from a computerized hook-up with airport arrivals and departures indicators to a daily exchange of pages with London. In Chicago, Field went one better and "imported" two CEEFAX chief sub-editors to help introduce the first proper commercial teletext service in the U.S. Other work, some of it also breaking new teletext frontiers, has been going on in Holland, Scandinavia, Switzerland and West Germany.

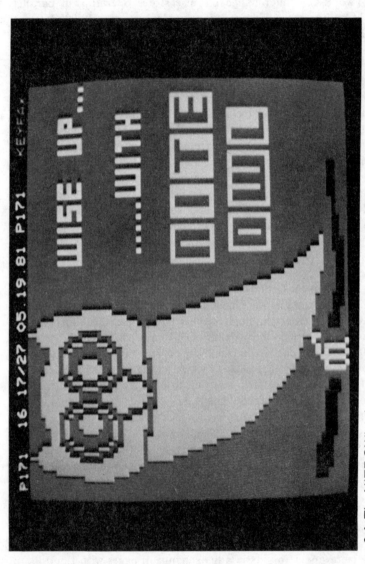

Figure 6.1. The NITE OWL teletext service provides viewers with the latest international, national and local news, weather, sports entertainment, travel and financial information. Courtesy Field Enterprises, Inc.

EDITORIAL CONTENT

Whatever system is used to transmit teletext, its value is only as good as its editorial content. Early critics had described teletext as an engineer's solution in search of a problem. In fact, the engineers' predictions as to its possible uses were accurate and foresighted. They saw not only the obvious uses such as news, sports results, stock market prices and the weather, but predicted its value in such matters as travel information, consumer interests, farming prices and details of television and radio programs.

The pattern again was radio. Teletext was soon offering many of the familiar features of radio, not at fixed times of the day to suit the schedules of the broadcaster, but all day long, to suit the choice of each individual viewer. This element of *choice* is one of the hardest to communicate to members of the public who have not had the opportunity to use teletext comfortably at home. It is choice as to subject, time and the order of importance. In fact, each viewer is in effect compiling his own individual news and information bulletin. It is the viewer who decides that he need never read another story about prison riots or the divorces of film stars.

The BBC-1 CEEFAX magazine, since it is on the BBC's main network, emphasizes hard news and results. It is here that the viewer seeks news headlines and a complete index of all news stories; a whole section on sports from football and cricket to horse racing and tennis, rugby league and badminton; and a wealth of business information from stock prices and reports on the commodity markets to company reports and currency exchange rates. BBC-1 CEEFAX also carries all the latest weather and travel information, from regularly updated weather maps of Britain to road news, train travel changes and seat availability statistics for the main airlines flying out of Heathrow (see Figure 6.2).

BBC-2 CEEFAX (Figure 6.3) at present is primarily an entertainment magazine. This is partly because the BBC's second network is not on the air throughout the whole day, but is on reduced hours in the morning as an economy measure. However, as teletext only needs a test card to ride piggy back on, BBC-2 CEEFAX is available for many more hours than BBC-2 programs are.

The entertainment content includes book, record, movie and theater reviews; schedules for art galleries, exhibitions, concert halls and trade shows; and features on hobbies and special interests. One of the most popular sections is fun and games where a series of puzzles, quizzes and competitions is available. There is also a section of jokes sent in by young viewers: elephant jokes, waiter-waiter jokes and terrible puns. There is

Figure 6.2 Contents Page from CEEFAX BBC 1

Ceefax on BBC 1

Contents: Page 100.

NEWS

Headlines	101
News in detail	102-116
News diary	117
People in the News	118
Charivari - a lighter look at the News	119
News Index	190
Newsreel	199

FINANCE

Headlines/Index	120
News and Reports	121-126
Market Reports	127-129
FT Index	130
Stocks and Shares	131-133
Money Markets	134
Exchange Rates	135-136
Commodities	137-138
Diary	139

SPORT

Headlines	140
Sports News	141-159

CEEFAX provides a rapid service of news, results and background.

On Saturdays, Sport Plus takes over some of the Finance pages to provide full coverage of the sporting scene.

FOOD GUIDE

Headlines/Index	161
Shopping Basket	162
Meat Prices	163
Fish + Egg Prices	164
Vegetable Prices	165
Fruit Prices	166
Recipe	167
Farm News	168

ENTERTAINMENT

Today's TV - BBC 1	171
BBC 2	172
ITV	173
Radio Highlights	174
Films on TV	175
Top Forty plus Top Ten L.P.s	176
TV Choice	177
Tomorrow's TV	178
Viewers' Questions	179

WEATHER AND TRAVEL

Headlines/Index	180
Weather Maps	181
Weather Forecast	182
Temperatures	183
Travel News	184-188
Tourist Rates	189

NEWSFLASH 150

Turn to this page to watch television programmes - when something important happens a NEWSFLASH will appear on the picture.

ALARM CLOCK PAGE 160

This page can change every minute. It can also be used as a silent alarm clock. Turn to page 160 for instructions.

NO NEED TO SHOUT 169

A mini-magazine of news and views of particular interest to those with hearing difficulty.

SUB-TITLES 170

A small number of BBC programmes have experimental CEEFAX subtitles to help the deaf.

OTHER PAGES

News about CEEFAX	191
Transmitter News	196
Engineering Tests	197-198

FULL INDEX

A - F	193
G - O	194
P - Z	195

Figure 6.3 Contents Page from CEEFAX BBC 2

Ceefax on BBC 2

```
                    ORBIT INDEX:    PAGE 200

         INTO ORBIT - PICK OF THE NEW PAGES:    PAGE 201
```

NEWS BACKGROUND		FEATURES	
This is the section which looks at the main news stories, picks out the key facts, and explains them simply.		This is the place to look for new, interesting or unusual subjects. Hobbies, pastimes, places to go and things to see can be found here.	
Index	202	Index	251
Pages	203-209	Pages	252-259
FUN AND GAMES		CONSUMER	
Every week, a new selection of puzzles, jokes and quizzes to amuse the whole family.		News, views and advice on a range of topics in and around the home and garden	
Index	210	Index	261
Pages	211-219	Pages	262-269
FINANCE		TV & RADIO PLUS	
Pages of valuable advice for the saver - from tax tips to investment information.		TV and radio programmes together with news of forthcoming programmes and a look behind the scenes.	
Index	220	Index	279
Pages	221-229	Pages	271-278
SPECTRUM		REVIEWS	
A country-wide look at exhibitions, galleries and film news, together with a What's On guide.		This section covers a wide area - music, from punk to classical, as well as theatre, books and films.	
Index	230	Index	280
Pages	231-239	Pages	281-289
SPORT		CONTACT	
These pages cover tables and statistics as well as a look ahead to forthcoming events.		A look at some of the organisations offering help to the public including addresses and telephone numbers.	
Index	240	Index	290
Pages	241-249	Pages	291-293

OTHER PAGES			
Newsflash	250	Subtitle	270
Alarm Clock	260	Index	295

even a graffiti wall where a selection of clean and political graffiti can be read.

The entertainment element is probably the most interesting development in what was originally considered an information medium. The CEEFAX editors were certain that what the public expects from a television set is *entertainment*. Viewers are interested in the news and want their own particular sports results instantly, but after that they look to the television set to entertain the family. For every viewer who is panting to dial up the historical details of the Battle of Lexington or to be informed about the average weight of the Australian dingo dog, there are 98 others who want to be amused. They don't mind if the gags have a dreadful schoolboy familiarity, or the word games are quite easy to solve—they turn to them.

This side of BBC-2 CEEFAX will almost certainly expand and develop. One way is via competitions or quizzes with prizes, which have proved popular. Four thousand viewers wrote in for cards to take part in Christmas bingo, and the top prize was only a couple of BBC records.

Many of the quizzes and games involve the use of the "reveal" facility. This allows an editor to hide a word, phrase or number in the text, which is only revealed when the individual viewer presses a button on his own keypad to make the answer appear. In addition to entertainment, this facility has obvious uses in educational programmed learning.

CAPTIONING FOR THE DEAF

Despite teletext's origin as a system of providing closed captions for the deaf, this group of viewers was actually a bit neglected in the first years of teletext broadcasting. News, sports results and business information, all features with broad appeal, were seen as the way to get the general public interested in and hooked on teletext, and they received the intense promotion needed to get the service accepted. Nevertheless, many hard-of-hearing people were among the early buyers of teletext, and they quickly began to make their views known.

There are many points of dispute over the best way to do captioning; one, for example, involves the central question of whether captions should aim to give the full text of a program, or only clues or a summary of the dialog. Deaf viewers have consistently asked for *more* programs with subtitles, whatever standards of consistency or technical accuracy have to be sacrificed to achieve quantity. And, of course, the great advantage of teletext subtitling is that it is non-intrusive, as the only ones who will be watching these subtitles are the deaf.

There are more than 2.5 million people in Britain with hearing problems.

These range from the 15,000 or so who were born deaf and cannot even articulate words properly, to about 100,000 who are totally deaf or very dependent on hearing aids, to 800,000 at the other end of the scale, who are afflicted with the failing hearing of old age. Given this spectrum of symptoms, it is not surprising that the deaf are far from unanimous about what type of subtitles should be used, and on what programs.

Some programs are inherently more suitable for captioning than others: a nature documentary with a simple running commentary will be easier to follow than a stand-up comedian who uses few visual gags. Nevertheless, one BBC comedy, "Yes, Minister," about goings-on in the Civil Service, proved extremely popular with the deaf, even though there were some 500 subtitles in a half hour. This quantity went against almost all the accepted canons of subtitling, but the deaf wrote in great numbers to express their approval.

"Yes, Minister" was one of the BBC programs to receive full subtitling. A special captioning unit worked with a cassette and a script to provide a time-coded floppy disc, with every subtitle in its allotted place. The disc was then fed into the CEEFAX transmission system at the appropriate moment, and the computer did the rest. The BBC now has plans to greatly increase the subtitling of its television programs, and has set aside a large sum of money to establish a new captioning center at Glasgow, Scotland in 1983.

Another approach, called manual subtitling, stores captions for a short program or simple occasion in the CEEFAX computer. When a key is pressed in the newsroom, the captions are revealed in sequence to the deaf viewer tuned to page 170 (BBC-1) or page 270 (BBC-2).

Full subtitling is extremely labor-intensive. It still takes an experienced subtitler some 20 hours to caption a one hour program. Thus a subtitler on a normal working schedule will complete barely 90 minutes of programs in a week.

Less expensive ways of adding subtitles are by film synopses and by precis subtitling. The film synopsis merely consists of a half dozen pages giving the storyline of the program. Precis subtitling is a series of running clues to the action, particularly drawing attention to those things not readily understood without the sound.

The latest development is Palantype subtitling. A trained operator uses a mechanical shorthand machine (of the kind used to prepare court transcripts) which produces a data stream of symbols, the phonetic equivalent of the words spoken on television. These phonetic symbols are then fed into a small computer which has been given a 70,000 word vocabulary, and which recognizes the symbols received, turning them back into English text. The latter are then transmitted as teletext subtitles.

Palantype makes the most sense for live events, and it received its first, full, on-the-air trial for President Reagan's inaugural speech on January 20, 1981. The reception by deaf viewers was wholehearted and enthusiastic. They forgave transcription errors and a three-to-eight-second delay, for the chance to be, as one of them put it, "at a moment in history, on level terms with the hearing."

Palantype is still being evaluated. It too is labor-intensive, and involves the use of highly-trained operators. Without a foreknowledge of the script, a Palantypist can keep going with verbatim transcription for only about 20 to 30 minutes without a break. It is easier with some sporting events —such as Wimbledon or World Cup football—but nonetheless demands much discipline. However, until voice-recognition computers are available with wide enough vocabularies to handle normal speech, Palantype may be the best approach to subtitling for current affairs programs, speeches, talk shows and sports, while more conventional subtitling is used for programs already "in the can."

FUTURE DEVELOPMENTS OF TELETEXT IN BRITAIN

Both editorial and engineering progress will further develop teletext in the near future. All the additions will be compatible with existing U.K. teletext; there is no built-in obsolescence. Among the concrete developments which can be expected are:

1. Expansion of capacity to more lines.

Although the technical specification for teletext sets aside eight lines in both television fields for data, the present system uses only four of them so as not to upset older television receivers. The move to four lines from two at the end of 1981 allowed the broadcasters to halve the access time. Another increase in the lines used would allow even quicker access, if this was thought necessary, or more likely an increase in the number of pages offered. It could be that the extra lines would be used for special services, such as subtitling or locally-originated material. Using a full eight lines would allow the BBC to broadcast a thousand pages of information per channel, which is approximately the number of words that appear in a weekly issue of *Time* or *Newsweek*. Teletext capacity for the commercial broadcasters would also be greatly increased, with more space for advertisements and promotional material.

Still another technique for increasing capacity already exists in the time-coded or subcoded pages which can be transmitted at one-minute intervals all day, and captured by dialing an additional set of four digits.

2. Technical improvements to teletext.

U.K. teletext has published a five stage plan which incorporates all possible enhancements to teletext, while still preserving that compatibility between existing sets and the new enhanced versions. One immediate refinement would be a polyglot alphabet capable of displaying all the accents and special letters required for any Latin-based language. There have already been on-the-air broadcasts by the BBC of "picture teletext," the transmission of still color photographs, their quality only limited by the cost of the receiver and decoder.

The quality of teletext transmissions is a marketing decision. It is the manufacturer and the retailer who sell the sets to the public who will have to decide which level is financially viable. The broadcaster can do it all now.

3. Telesoftware.

One exciting development is telesoftware, which is the broadcasting of computer programs via teletext to home or personal computers. An experiment under the aegis of Brighton Polytechnic, with both the BBC and ITV participating, involved broadcasting computer programs to specially built microprocessors in a dozen schools. The BBC has taken this one step further by licensing a computer firm to build BBC microcomputers which will be teletext compatible. Telesoftware programs will then be downloaded directly into these machines as part of a larger scheme by the BBC to teach computer literacy to a mass audience. This will be achieved by means of TV programs, at-home learning and the home computer. The teletext compatibility will add about £100 to the cost of the microcomputer, which costs about £265.

CEEFAX will almost certainly establish its own "Computer Corner," both for assisting the computer literacy project, and for generally encouraging home computer hobbyists.

4. Computer-to-computer interfaces.

Another way in which computers will be integrated with teletext is to speed up the gathering and formatting of teletext pages by direct computer-to-computer connections. CEEFAX is already able to do this with stock market prices, and ORF in Vienna does it with airport arrival and departure information. CEEFAX has also established links with a computer in Britain's west country, which in an emergency could be an invaluable means of communication between rescue services, as well as a way of keeping the public informed. As more and more information is stored in computerized data bases, such connections are bound to grow in importance.

5. Regionalization of teletext.

ORACLE has already begun regionalizing its service, inputting teletext information directly from its different companies at a local level, and thus giving teletext much more local information—and much more local advertising. ITV has issued its first advertising rate card, and early indications are that the advertisers are very interested. In 1982 a message running on ORACLE for a week cost the advertiser £400.

THE WAY AHEAD

There is no doubt in Britain that teletext is here to stay. There is every sign that within a year or so almost every new television set coming off the production line will be equipped to receive teletext. The fall in the price of teletext has been considerable, and it will soon be cheaper to include the necessary equipment than to leave it out when manufacturing television sets.

From the broadcaster's point of view, teletext suits the rhythm of television; it can update program guides on talk shows, correct mistakes and add subtitles to each network's programs. It can be seen as a weapon helping the broadcaster maintain his control over that television set in the corner of the living room.

For years the broadcaster has looked on the TV set as his property, the last link in a chain that begins in the television studio. Now, as a result of modern technologies, that TV set has become a playback and recording device, or a display terminal for a home computer. The viewer has become his own program planner, choosing from a variety of program sources, as well as pay TV, cable or satellite networks.

Teletext is one of the few inventions that is entirely broadcast-related. It can be used to enhance the service given by the broadcaster to his public and to directly respond to viewers' concerns and interests. In an era that sees broadcasting becoming more and more inflexible, more and more dominated by computer-scheduling and audience ratings, teletext is a return to the excitement and immediacy of old-fashioned broadcasting. It is also cheap, simple and gives the customer what he or she wants—very quickly.

7

Videotext in Canada

by Blaise Downey

INTRODUCTION

Canada has developed the first of what is known as "second generation" interactive videotext technologies—and at the cost of considerably less government investment than either of its two closest competitors, the U.K. and France. The system, called Telidon, is one in which the user can have a kind of conversation with a central computer, with answers coming back in both pictures and text on an adapted home television set.

As in other videotext systems, contents pages or menus guide users through a tree-structured search technique. Or if they already know where to find the information, they simply key in the page number directly. Each terminal is identified by an address code so that subscribers can be billed for material they request. Some data is provided at no charge, such as advertising or government information. Videotext is typically used for providing information with a longer life than teletext information—for example, reference material for business and education, statistics and entertainment such as video games. The videotext terminal accepts a wide range of peripheral devices to allow it to serve as a full-fledged computer.

Telidon also refers to teletext—the one-way access to data banks by a mass audience. That means that any individual with the necessary hardware in his home or office can call up desired information using a small keypad. The resulting images can be seen on home television sets, desktop monitors in offices, or large-screen projectors. Teletext programs generally carry a file of timely general interest information broadcast in cycle, or specific information at given times. The available data are typically updateable items like news, weather, sports, community notes, stock listings and advertising. The menus are typically much smaller than the information retrievable over a videotext system with its much more extensive memory. The information in the Telidon system can be carried to and from individuals and computer data bases over any communications medium—the telephone network's paired copper wires, video cables, optical fibers, microwave, satellite or whatever transmission systems the future may hold.

Telidon was first introduced in 1978, after several years of research, by the Communications Research Centre of the federal Department of Communications (DOC) in Ottawa. Sometimes referred to as "two-way television," it is a sophisticated and flexible communications system that uses microprocessor-based terminals to generate color displays of text and graphics.

Sophisticated Graphics Capability

As discussed in Chapter 2, two types of graphic displays are used in videotext systems—alphamosaic or alphageometric. The former, used in the British Prestel and French Antiope services, describes a graphic process similar to that found in satellite photographs from LANDSAT or in the crude images of a video game. They are composed of a pattern of squares, known as building blocks.

With the more sophisticated "second generation" alphageometric method employed in Telidon, a combination of points, lines, arcs, rectangular areas and polygons can produce a more refined image. The result is similar to the colored picture on a magazine cover which is composed of a screen of minute overlying dots of different colors. (The 525-line mesh on a standard North American TV screen produces a rough image, however, compared to the 130 or so dots in most magazine reproductions.) In addition, Telidon can transmit photographs using a TV camera to scan the image, and then converting it into digital form for storage and transmission.

The relative refinement of the Telidon image, compared to its predecessors, has already been a selling factor and will become increasingly important as the system is applied to an expanding array of uses. With Telidon, for example, one may produce accurate curves on graphs, detailed architectural drawings, exact wiring diagrams and plans for industrial pipe and conduit layouts, precise weather maps or drawings of houses for real estate listings. The alphageometric method also lends itself to reproduction of such cursive alphabets as Chinese, Arabic or Inuit (Eskimo). In transmission, these languages can appear on the screen either vertically, or from right to left, according to customary usage.

THE ECONOMICS OF TELIDON

Manufacturers' Investment

The principal manufacturer of Telidon terminals is Norpak Ltd. This electronics firm started out in 1975 as a comparatively small organization in the tiny rural community of Pakenham, located 40 miles west of Ottawa. Largely as a result of its close cooperation with the DOC in the development and manufacture of Telidon equipment, the company has mushroomed, now employing 300 people, with a new plant in Ottawa proper. Norpak's total sales for the year ending March 1982, totalled roughly $20 million, a 100% increase over the previous year.

The two other principal manufacturers, working under licensing agreements with Norpak, are Electrohome Ltd. of Kitchener, Ontario and AEL Microtel Ltd. of Burnaby, British Columbia, the manufacturing arm of British Columbia Telephone (a subsidiary of General Telephone and Electronics). Another Ottawa firm, Hemton Corporation, has worked closely with Norpak since its inception two years ago on the graphic capabilities of Telidon. In December 1981, Norpak acquired 100% of the shares of Hemton.

Canada's largest telephone utility, Bell Canada, has a long-standing interest in Telidon. Its equipment manufacturing subsidiary, Northern Telecom, is producing the terminals for the VISTA field trial discussed later in this chapter. Bell-Northern Research, their jointly-owned research and development facility and Canada's largest non-government research organization, is another of the 40 or so Canadian firms that has made major contributions to Telidon. Many of the biggest names in Canadian electronics—Mitel Corporation, Digital Equipment of Canada, Gandalf Technologies Inc., Nabu Manufacturing Corporation, Socioscope Inc., Systemhouse Ltd. and The Genesys Group—have realized the potential of Telidon and are involved in some facet of the business. Mitel, for example, supplies the microprocessor chip based on very large-scale integrated (VLSI) logic. In all, several thousand jobs are directly or indirectly attributable to Telidon, and this number will increase considerably if initial domestic and international interest in the system is translated into major sales of Canadian equipment worldwide.

Major financing of Norpak, to the tune of about $30 million, has come from the highly diversified Noranda Mines Ltd. through its subsidiary Maclaren Power and Paper Co. The federal government, through DOC, has committed an additional $45 million to be used through 1983. Speculation is that Norpak will go public with a share offering in early 1983. By the end of 1983, total investment by the private industry sector will have reached an additional $200 million.

Commercial Applications

With the technology so new, there are not yet many commercial applications of Telidon, although several are being developed. There are, however, a large number of field trials under way or planned for the near future in Canada and abroad, some of considerable scope. As of spring 1982 there were 52 field trials under way in Canada alone, many of them nonprofit educational projects. Table 7.1 lists the trials and commercial services currently under way.

The first Telidon trial started in January 1980, and was sponsored by the Ontario Educational Communications Authority. Fifty-five Telidon terminals throughout Ontario received teletext transmissions via TV Ontario (an educational TV network in that province) and Anik B satellite. It also had videotext capacity via the telephone network. The western part of Canada became involved later in 1980 when videotext was transmitted over coaxial cable to 33 terminals as part of Manitoba Telephone System's Project Ida. The largest field trial to date has been Bell Canada's Project VISTA which began in May 1981, with 500 terminals in Toronto and in the outskirts of Quebec City. Over 70,000 "pages" of information are available over this system. Bell Canada has invested $8.5 million in VISTA, with the federal government contributing an additional $2.5 million, mainly for terminal hardware. Experiments with videotext over optical fibers (long, extremely fine strands of glass that transmit light signals at far greater volume than conventional signals on ordinary wire or coaxial cable) form part of Manitoba Tel's Project Elie, introducing Telidon in a rural environment. Other projects are under way, or are scheduled in the near future, in British Columbia, Alberta, Saskatchewan and Nova Scotia.

The Canadian videotext industry is now embarking on the "make or break" commercial exploitation stage. At stake are world markets potentially worth billions of dollars—if consumers accept the new technology—which can bring banking, shopping, electronic mail, education and up-to-the-minute news directly into the home. But the industry faces two challenges in tapping consumer markets: reducing the cost of the terminals and decoder units; and developing content that consumers are willing to buy. Terminal prices now range from $800 to $1200 depending on the type and features included, a price considered too high for the average business or individual user.

The International Market

The international market for Telidon looks promising. Communications Minister Francis Fox summed up that aspect of the industry when he spoke of the adoption by the American Telephone and Telegraph Company (AT&T) and Columbia Broadcasting System (CBS) of standards compatible with Telidon: "Telidon now forms the heart of the North American videotext standard adopted by some of the largest communications companies and electronics manufacturers in the world ... for applications ranging from electronic magazine publishing to home banking and reservation services."[1] He also said that sales agreements with West Germany have been made which will be worth at least $15 million to Canadian companies during the next few years. The technology is also being used in Switzerland, England and Australia, and by the governments of Venezuela and the United States. Also, Fox added, "French and British governments are contributing to Telidon projects in Canada. The French consulate in Montreal, for example, has created a number of pages on subjects such as French films, wines and lifestyles."

Along similar lines, an international Telidon service called Novatex has also begun operating in several Canadian embassies and consulates. It is designed to serve businesses and government agencies operating internationally by providing information on such topics as trade regulations, statistics, geography, agriculture and energy. In Venezuela, most of the field trial terminals are in storefront locations throughout Caracas so that the average citizen can access the data bank. It is Telidon's equivalent of the pay phone, and may point the way of the future in developing countries —even if some people cannot afford the terminals, they can still benefit from the system.

CONTENT

Any system such as Telidon is only as good as its data base—the information it makes available to customers. Three Canadian companies in particular have been most active in developing pages of information and data base design: Infomart Ltd., a joint subsidiary of Torstar Corporation (owner of Canada's largest circulation daily newspaper *The Toronto Star)* and of Southam Inc., a major newspaper chain; Hemton Corporation; and Dominion Directory Company Ltd. of Burnaby, British Columbia. The challenge now is to develop useful information data banks on news, business, tourism, entertainment, culture, education and other topics both for Canada and for a world market. In the U.S., Times Mirror of Los Angeles and Time Inc. are the principal suppliers of information to Telidon systems. The Times Mirror group has also undertaken a $1 million field trial of Telidon which began in March 1982 with 350 terminals in Los Angeles-area homes.

Table 7.1: Domestic and International Telidon Trials and Commercial Services

Project/Operator	Location	Operation	Number of Terminals	Transmission Medium
Project AGT-TELIDON/ Alberta Government Telephone	Calgary, Alberta	August 1981	30	Telephone circuit
ELECTRONIC MESSAGE SERVICE/ British Columbia Telephone	Vancouver, British Columbia	December 1981	125	Telephone circuit
Project ELIE/ Manitoba Telephone System	Elie, Manitoba	September 1981	150	Optical fiber
Project IDA/ Manitoba Telephone System	South Headingley, Manitoba	June 1980	33	Coaxial cable
Project INFOCABLE/Cable Telecommunication Research Institute	Brockville, Ontario	September 1982	500	Coaxial cable
Maritime Telephone and Telegraph Trial	Nova Scotia	March 1982	15	Telephone circuit
Project MERCURY/ New Brunswick Telephone Co.	Saint John, New Brunswick	April 1981	45	Telephone circuit (dedicated)

Table 7.1: Domestic and International Telidon Trials and Commercial Services (cont'd.)

Project/Operator	Location	Operation	Number of Terminals	Transmission Medium
Project CANTEL/Task Force on Services to the Public	Across Canada	April 1981	100	Telephone circuit
Project PATHFINDER/ Saskatchewan Telecommunications	Regina, Saskatchewan	June 1982	100	Telephone circuit
Project IRIS/Canadian Broadcasting Corporation	Toronto, Ontario Montrial, Quebec Calgary, Alberta	September 1982	700	Broadcast
Telidon and Education Project/ TV Ontario	Across Ontario	1) March 1979 2) January 1980	55	1) Telephone 2) Broadcast
Telidon 2/Télécâble-Videotron	Montreal, Quebec	1) Spring 1981 2) Spring 1982	1) 250 2) 250	1) Teletext-coaxial cable 2) Videotext-coaxial cable
Project VISTA/ Bell Canada	Toronto, Ontario Montreal & Quebec City, Quebec	May 1981	491	Telephone circuit

Table 7.1: Domestic and International Telidon Trials and Commercial Services (cont'd.)

Project/Operator	Location	Operation	Number of Terminals	Transmission Medium
Project INET/CCG/TCTS	Across Canada	July 1982	400	Datapac
Project CABOT/ Memorial University of Newfoundland	Newfoundland	July 1982	3	Telephone
Project GRASSROOTS/ Infomart and MTS	Southern Manitoba	May 1981	100	Telephone circuit (dedicated)
Teleguide to Ontario/ Infomart	Toronto, Ontario	May 1982	2000	Telephone circuit
Marketfax/Cableshare	Canada	November 1981	12	X.25 Digital network
Videopress/Cableshare	London, Ontario	November 1981	6 interactive; 6 non-interactive	
Venezuela Telidon System/ Infomart	Caracas, Venezuela	Early 1981	25	Telephone circuit
WETA-AMC Teletext Trial	Washington, DC	May 1981	64	Broadcast off-air

Table 7.1: Domestic and International Telidon Trials and Commercial Services (cont'd.)

Project/Operator	Location	Operation	Number of Terminals	Transmission Medium
Bakersfield Telidon Trial	San Joaquin Valley, CA	October 1982	500	Telephone circuit
Myer Emporium Telidon Trial	Melbourne, Australia	TBD	TBD	
Project NOVATEX/Teleglobe	International	February 1982	67	Telephone network
Time Inc. Teletext Trial	Orlando, FL San Diego, CA	July 1982	300	Satellite & coaxial cable
Times Mirror Videotex Services	Southern California	March 1982	150-cable 200-phone	Telephone & coaxial cable

Source: Telidon Field Trials Directorate, Department of Communications, Ottawa, Ontario, February 1982.

Pierre Juneau, former deputy minister of communications, once said: "The most fundamental question of all, of course, is content. How do we encourage the creation of the truly diverse information sources required by a bilingual, regionalized nation that spans a continent? Can we establish an economically viable information industry in Canada, or will the technology which we have developed be used by publishers in other countries to overwhelm our own content providers? Or have we sold a better mousetrap to the world, only to find that we have become the mice?"[2]

Doug Parkhill, head of research for DOC and the senior government official responsible for the successful development of Telidon, adds this thought: "It's like the chicken-and-egg situation. We need to provide content to get consumers to buy the system, but you need people to buy the system to know what kind of content to develop."[3] One could add, to ensure that the expensive creation of content will be economically attractive to the information providers in the first place.

Infomart has led the industry by developing a videotext service called "Grassroots" which focuses on agriculture and the particular farming needs of Manitoba province. Subscribers pay $47.50 a month to lease terminals and five cents a minute to use the system, and receive up-to-date information on such things as weather conditions and commodity exchange prices. This service has been sold to Frittsco of California, and Infomart will assist that company to adapt the contents to applications in the rich San Joaquin Valley.

Toward the end of 1981, Montreal saw the introduction of the world's first Telidon cable newspaper. This service was developed by the Videtron group of cable companies and by *La Presse,* one of the largest circulation French language dailies in the world. The paper has assigned a special editorial staff to create a Telidon newspaper for more than half a million subscribers.

A $6 million program, jointly funded by the federal government and the Canadian Broadcasting Corporation (CBC), called Project Iris, will soon provide weather, news, sports, shopping and financial information. Meanwhile, the independent nationwide network, CTV, has already been running a Telidon weather report. On camera, the announcer stands in front of a TV screen, holding a keypad. By punching the correct buttons, he can instantly call up detailed maps of Canada in contrasting colors, provincial boundaries, temperatures at major centers, isobars connecting places with the same barometric pressure and shaded areas that roll across the prairies or out to the Atlantic provinces, and focus on different regions of the country in even greater detail.

CONCLUSION

In addition to its superior graphics capability and advanced micropro-cessor technology, Telidon has built into its design flexibility with regard to methods of transmission—a virtual hedge against obsolescence. Herb Bown, now vice president of corporate development for Norpak Ltd., was with DOC during the development years and has been described as the "Father of Telidon." Commenting on the need to keep information storage separate from delivery and receiving systems, he said, "We were deter-mined not to make Telidon terminals dependent in any way on the communications media or on the receiving display hardware ... Existing communications are constantly being improved—with fiber optics, satellite and other broadband services. We know the resolution of TV itself may well be improved, or TV may even be replaced by a totally new display technology. The additional electronics we're putting into a TV to allow it to display this new alphanumeric, graphic and tonal image material will also change rapidly with advances in microprocessors and memory system and large-scale integration."[4]

Without the separation of data from hardware, Bown explained, "we would have been stuck with a data life expectancy of about five years before much of the information in data banks would have to be redone for the next generations of systems. That's one area where our approach is definitely superior," he concluded.

So the technology of tomorrow is with us today, and Canada is right on top of it. Telidon has certainly arrived on the market at an appropriate time.

NOTES

1. Communications Minister Francis Fox, in a speech to the International Information/ Word Processing Association, Ottawa, Canada (December 1, 1981).

2. Communications Deputy Minister Pierre Juneau, in a speech at the annual meeting of the Videotex Information Service Providers' Associa-tion of Canada (VISPAC), Ottawa, Canada (November 23, 1981).

3. *The Citizen* (Ottawa, Canada) March 23, 1982.

4. *Telidon* (Ottawa, Canada: Federal Department of Communications) May 1981.

8

Videotext in France

by Efrem Sigel

"The market is there," said the official of SOFRATEV, the French agency responsible for marketing television communications systems abroad, pointing to a wall map of North America. "In some ways," he confided, "France is still an underdeveloped country."

The remarks of Jean-Pierre Teyssier, general manager of SOFRATEV, made to a visiting American in the fall of 1980, are a revealing insight into the French approach to "telematique," a made-up word for the combination of computer and telecommunications technology as reflected in teletext and videotext. For the aggressive French push to develop and export this technology contrasts with the still-rudimentary state of its exploitation in France itself. And the French telephone system, although the beneficiary of enormous state investment since the mid-1970s, still lags behind that of a number of other Western countries in extent and quality of service.

There is no denying the innovations of the French in videotext systems. One example was the development of Antiope with its parallel attribute system of coding digital information for broadcast transmission, which resulted in a flexible yet economic system for broadcast teletext. In use in France since 1977, it has been the object of a growing number of tests in international markets. In the U.S. alone, TV stations owned by CBS, NBC and Westinghouse, along with various public stations, have experimented with a U.S. version of Antiope since 1979. In 1980, CBS had enough confidence in the merits of the technology to propose its adoption by the FCC as a U.S. broadcast standard. (A year later, after AT&T had announced its videotext Presentation Level Protocol, and after the French had announced modifications of Antiope to meet this standard, CBS amended its filing to cover this "extended Antiope" format.)

Another example is the leap of French terminal manufacturers into mass production of small black and white video screens for viewdata display. Spurred on by the promise of a large, subsidized national market for this equipment, companies like Thomson, CIT Alcatel, Telic and Matra developed prototypes and confidently prepared the long production runs that would justify wholesale prices of just a few hundred dollars. By 1981 these manufacturers had obtained several preliminary commitments from U.S. customers, though not in the large quantities they had hoped for. Tymshare, for example, agreed to import and distribute to its customers a terminal made by Matra. The Model 415, introduced in February 1982, has automatic computer log-in, built-in modem and automatic dialer, and sells for $649. (See Figure 8.1.)

BACKGROUND OF VIDEOTEXT IN FRANCE

Both the broadcast and telephone-line videotext services in France are the result of research conducted at the Centre Commun d'Etudes de Télévision et Télécommunication (CCETT) (joint research center for television and telecommunication). This research institute was established in 1972 to serve the state-owned broadcasting and telecommunications authorities. In 1973 the CCETT began studying teletext, seeking data coding and transmission formats that would permit greater flexibility than the British CEEFAX system.

The Antiope broadcast teletext system that resulted was intended to work with both 525-line (U.S. and Japanese) and 625-line (European) broadcasting standards, and to be equally useful whether the teletext magazine was limited to several lines of the picture (100 to 200 pages) or whether it employed the entire channel, (thus permitting 5000 to 6000 pages).

Antiope was also designed to be compatible with the interactive telephone-based videotext system known as Teletel. Research on Teletel was also conducted at Rennes during the early and mid-1970s at the instigation of the Direction Générale des Télécommunications (DGT), the French telecommunications authority. Teletext trials began in France in 1977, and by 1978 SOFRATEV had undertaken an ambitious effort to get the technology accepted in other countries, principally the U.S. However, experiments with Teletel did not get underway until 1981.

STATUS OF TELETEXT IN FRANCE

By early 1981, nine teletext services were in operation, though the number of teletext decoders installed in all of France was between 4000 and 5000 according to a spokesman at Antiope. Most of the information

Figure 8.1 The Model 415 viewdata terminal, manufactured by Matra, features user programmable function keys and a 9-inch diagonal screen that can handle 24 lines of text and occupies only one square foot of space. Courtesy Tymshare.

was produced by various national and regional government agencies, though a few private companies or agencies were also sponsoring a particular service. Among the better known teletext programs are:

- *Antiope-Antenne 2*. Some 60 to 100 pages of news, TV program listings and practical information produced by the editorial staff of Antenne 2, one of the government-owned channels, and broadcast 14 hours a day throughout the country. Teletext pages are also broadcast on the full channel four hours a week so that viewers without teletext decoders can also have access to the service.

- *Antiope-Bourse*. This program, put together by the Chambre Syndicale des agents de change (association of money-changers) consists of stock prices, money rates and foreign exchange rates, all stored in a computer at the Paris Bourse. About a quarter of the 330 pages available contain foreign conversion rates or economic data. (See Figure 8.2.)

- *Antiope-Meteo*. This service consists of 40 pages of weather information compiled by computers at the national weather service.

- *Antiope-Route*. Provided by the Centre Regional d'Information et de Coordination Routieres, this service, also occupying 40 pages, offers reports on traffic delays, advice on the best vacation routes, and other useful information for travelers.

STATUS OF TELEPHONE VIDEOTEXT SERVICES IN FRANCE

The two major telephone-based videotext experiments underway in France in the early 1980s were the Teletel 3V project in Velizy, and the electronic telephone directory trial in Rennes, in the province of Ille-et-Vilaine.

Teletel 3V Project

The Velizy trial, which began in July 1981, involved 2500 households in five suburbs located to the southwest of Paris: Velizy, Versailles, Buc, Jouy-en-Josas and Les Loges en Josas. Three different terminals were installed for the trial: 1) an adaptor connected to an existing TV set, capable of communicating with the central computer; 2) an adaptor also equipped to receive broadcast teletext transmissions; 3) a standalone terminal able to communicate with the computer, but not attaching to the

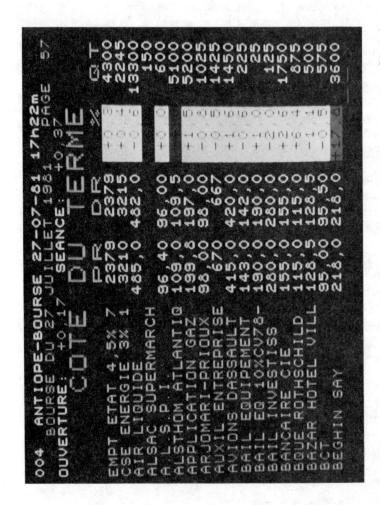

Figure 8.2 Antiope-Bourse, a teletext program developed by the Chambre Syndicale des agents de change, gives viewers information on exchange rates and other economic news. Courtesy Sofratev.

TV set. All terminals used in the test had full alphanumeric keyboards, and incorporated a modem capable of transmitting computer-to-terminal signals at 1200 bits per second (bps), and terminal-to-computer signals at 75 bps.

The DGT, organizer of the trial, decided not to levy a charge for using the service during the test, except for a telephone usage fee of half a franc for each five minutes of service. Information providers were permitted to charge for their information if they wished, though most chose not to do so.

The computer center at Velizy consisted of a network of seven minicomputers capable of handling 300 calls simultaneously. To allow IPs in distant locations to supply information from their own computers, the center simply routed the call to the proper computer, via the French data transmission network, TRANSPAC. More than 40 public agencies and more than 100 private organizations supplied information, including local and regional government agencies, insurance companies, banks, newspaper and publishing companies, etc. Figure 8.3 shows a typical page from the Velizy trial.

The Teletel 3V project began with a data base of 60,000 pages. The list of information providers was very wide-ranging; among the organizations participating were mail order companies, automobile manufacturers, banks, tour operators, food manufacturers, airline companies, railroads, schools, newspapers and magazines.

Some of the specific kinds of information and transactions services offered were the following:

- news and sports results

- timetables for 1500 French trains

- stock quotations

- listings of industries, tradesmen and organizations in 38,000 French cities, towns and villages

- merchandise offerings from mail order houses

- travel and hotel listings

- government-supplied information about consumers, education, taxes, health and transportation

- an electronic mailbox feature enabling users to send messages to one another

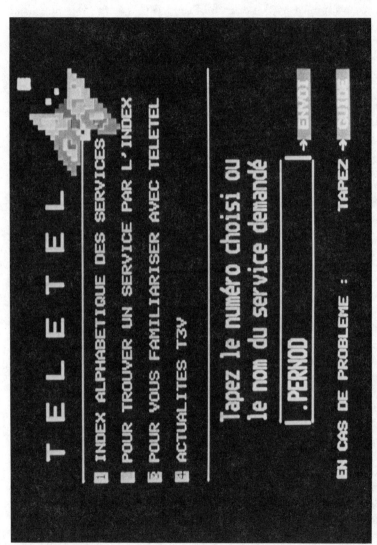

Figure 8.3 Participants in the Velizy trial use menu pages such as this one to select information or services they require. Courtesy Young & Associates, Inc.

Participants in the Teletel 3V project were selected after notifying all telephone subscribers in the region about the test, and obtaining nearly 8000 applications. The final sample reflected an attempt to give particular representation to those with above-average education and income. A breakdown supplied by P. Leclercq of the DGT, is as follows: industrial managers and professionals, 7%; merchants and artisans, 7%; supervisors and managers, 23.5%; middle-level employees and skilled workers, 23.5%, white-collar employees, 13%; workers, 13%; retired people, 13%.

Volunteers for the service were asked in advance how they expected to use it. Among the features most often requested were administrative information (mentioned by 80% of the volunteers), reservations (78%) and banking information (75%).

A variety of French companies participated by supplying equipment or communications services for the Velizy experiment. Matra and Thomson provided terminals; Steria, Matra and Cii Honeywell Bull supplied computer and communications equipment for the information center; Telesystems and CAP Sogeti Gemini provided links to remote computers.

The Teletel 3V trial was to run until the end of 1982. Besides statistics to be generated automatically by the Teletel center and by remote computers, the DGT was also conducting field interviews and special studies to gauge reaction to the service on the part of the participants.

Growth of Bank Participation

The swift growth of bank participation in videotext services is a recent phenomenon that is likely to pick up momentum. One example is the favorable reaction of one participant in the Velizy trial, the Credit Commercial de France (CCF), which has lead to the adoption of Teletel videotext as an affordable means of improving their banking services. The videotext service, called Videobanque, offers 24-hour financial services to major corporate clients. All of CCF's branches in Paris can handle Teletel transactions and 60 other offices are expected to have terminals by September 1982.

The terminals, known as Minitels (essentially the same hardware used in the electronic directory project described below) have been installed in 18 corporations with another 25 scheduled for service. These businesses pay a fee of $60 to $300 depending on the number and type of accounts to be accessed.

CCF plans to provide information on foreign exchange rates, stock quotations and intra-company and inter-branch transfers by fall 1982.

Electronic Directory Assistance Project

The Ille-et-Vilaine experiment, with electronic directory assistance terminals, is the most ambitious experiment undertaken by any telephone or telecommunications company. The original plan was to supply small black and white terminals to all 275,000 telephone subscribers in Ille-et-Vilaine, as the first step in an attempt to convert 30 million French telephone subcribers to electronic retrieval by 1992. The purpose was two-fold: 1) to do away with the costly printing of paper directories, and to greatly reduce the expense of a directory-assistance service employing 6000 operators around France; and 2) to develop an indigenous French manufacturing industry producing electronic terminals in enormous quantity, and thus storming world markets with the devices.

The data base for the Ille-et-Vilaine project included all white page directory listings for the region (over 250,000) plus yellow page information. The latter included paid advertising from companies that were logical users of the service, such as hotels, restaurants and retailers.

Although installation of the first 1500 terminals began in May 1981, an important modification was instituted under the new government of President François Mitterand. The newly appointed director-general of telecommunications, Jacques Dondoux, announced that no longer would acceptance of the terminals be obligatory; subscribers would have the choice of the electronic version or the existing paper directory.

(An indication of this change in attitude was given by the Secretary of State for Post, Telecommunications and Television, Louis Mexandeau, in the inauguration of the Teletel 3V trial. He stated that the government would not impose acceptance of a new technology but that "our politics aim, on the contrary, at the creation of telematics applications that would be guided by public opinion and judgment.")

Although the change in plan reflects the political and practical reality that the average citizen will not discard the habits of a lifetime overnight, it did call into question the underlying assumptions of a mass conversion to the age of electronic information retrieval. As *The Economist* said in its October 19, 1981 issue, allowing subscribers a choice means that the French telephone company "will still have to provide the costly paper directories that the electronic terminals were intended to replace." Not only that, but would the manufacturing of the terminals themselves be economical: "for the project to succeed," the magazine noted, "the telecoms industry must have an assured mass market. Otherwise, hopes of producing the terminals at a price of $100 each will be smashed. And the ultimate aim of getting videotex into the French home may miss its target."

FUTURE OF VIDEOTEXT IN FRANCE

By dint of large-scale investment in modernization of its antiquated telephone network, France by the late 1970s had created Europe's largest market for telecommunications equipment. The telematique program, conceived of as a vast leap forward into the age of information processing, hoped to build on this level of investment to foster an indigenous industry strong in electronics, computers and telecommunications.

Far from braking this ambitious program, the Mitterand government has attempted to accelerate it. Government funding for research and development in computers, set at $270 million in 1981, was to increase to $350 million in 1982 out of a total government R&D budget of $6 billion. The telephone network, which went from 7 million to 16 million main phone lines between 1975 and 1980, is now converting to digital exchanges at a rapid rate; 85% of new exchanges ordered in 1981 were digital and the figure in 1982 was to be 92%, according to Maurice Bernard of the Centre National d'Etudes de Telecommunications.

However, modernizing a telephone network for the purpose of better serving existing voice and data needs is one thing. Grafting onto that network an entirely new mission, namely getting millions of citizens to use terminals for information retrieval, is an entirely different matter. The French could, of course, turn out to be more eager users of computerized information services than the British, the Americans, the Germans and others who have tried out two-way videotext services; if the French rush to adopt this new form of communication, the market may blossom as planned. But if old habits die hard and the cost of providing videotext services turns out to be far higher than expected, then all that the French will have accomplished will have been to waste far more money at a far faster rate than their competitors in the world of videotext.

A complicating factor, of course, is the political and business uncertainty prevailing in France as a result of the Socialist government's nationalization program. Several of the companies affected by this, including Thomson-Brandt, Matra and Saint Gobain, are themselves major suppliers of computer and communications equipment; the effect on future operations of these companies is yet to be worked out. More practically, the sums required to buy out these and other firms run into the billions of dollars. Even though the money is to come from long-term government bonds, the size of the commitments, when juxaposed with the government's other ambitious spending plans, raises the question of whether the government can afford to carry out all of its intentions. A slowdown would not be the first time that a theoretical plan for an advanced videotext service has run into the practical realities of money, consumer preferences and ingrained habits of information use.

9

Videotext in Other Countries

by Efrem Sigel

As the preceding chapters have shown, videotext has become a worldwide phenomenon with rapid growth particularly in the U.K., Canada and France. Research has led to the implementation of videotext and/or teletext systems in many other countries as well (see Table 1.1 in Chapter 1). These services are primarily in the experimental or trial stages although several countries expect to launch full-fledged services within the next year. The services are supported by the individual governments and by the PTT (Minister of Post and Telecommunications) of each country. Success hinges on the cooperation of government, local manufacturers and suppliers of equipment as well as IPs and users.

This chapter outlines the status of videotext and teletext services, as of June 1982, in most of the countries that are actively experimenting with them: Austria, Finland, Germany, Greece, Hungary, Italy, Japan, the Netherlands, Norway, Spain, Sweden and Switzerland.[1]

Although it is hard to predict the future of videotext internationally, it is safe to project that growth is inevitable. The technology alone holds an alluring charm for governments, PTTs, equipment manufacturers, IPs and others involved with telecommunications.

AUSTRIA

A videotext pilot trial has been operating in Austria since March 1981. As of June 1982, 20,000 pages of information were available and 100 IPs and 250 users were participating in the trial.

Nationwide access to the system is available at local telephone rates, making electronic message service cheaper than ordinary mail. The Austrian videotext service offers complete user-to-user messaging as well as information retrieval, booking and ordering service. The Austrian PTT plans to implement an experimental videotext network using external computers by the end of 1982, and by 1984 a full-fledged service should be in operation.

The PTT has also called for the development of an intelligent external decoder called MUPID (Multipurpose Universally Programmable Intelligent Decoder). It can easily convert standard television sets into videotext terminals and comes with a full ASCII keyboard. It also provides high quality graphics (both geometric and mosaic) and makes full use of telesoftware. Beginning in September 1982, MUPID can be rented from the PTT at a monthly fee of approximately $8 (U.S.).

FINLAND

The first viewdata trial in Finland was initiated in 1976. Using Prestel technology, but terminals manufactured locally, the system was run by one PDP-11 computer and had a data base of approximately 20,000 pages. The three major participants in the trial were Sanoma Corporation, the largest publishing organization in Helsinki, Helsinki Telephone Company and Nokia Electronics. This trial service, incorporating 30 terminals, cost between $600,000 and $700,000.

After the field trial was completed in March 1980, the three companies formed Helsinki Telset. This system is aimed at businesses although it is projected that, in the next three to five years, the home market will open up considerably. Helsinki Telset uses a double PDP-11/34 computer with a capacity of 80,000 pages.

Approximately 300 terminals were in use across the country as of February 1982. As of 1981, 10 more trials were planned with two already in operation in Turku and Tampere. By 1990, about 150,000 terminals are expected to be operating in homes throughout Finland. (No teletext service was operating in Finland as of May 1981.)

GERMANY

Next to the British Prestel service, the German Bildschirmtext trial is the largest functioning viewdata service in Europe—far larger than the Teletel project in Velizy, France, which has garnered so much publicity. Moreover, the German Bundespost, originator of the service, has also been a world pioneer in developing the so-called "gateway" facility whereby a videotext subscriber can be connected to a third-party computer to retrieve information. This innovation could well rank as the most important since the original idea of a simple videotext retrieval service.

Bildschirmtext was first demonstrated to the German public in 1977 at the International Radio Exhibition in Berlin, one of the world's foremost consumer electronics shows. The system on display was the British viewdata system. Following the exhibition, the Deutsche Bundespost began conducting private technical trials to adapt the technology to the needs of the German alphabet (by adding umlauts, for example) and to make other technical changes. By the 1979 Radio Exhibition, some 125 IPs were ready to show videotext pages.

Public field trials began in early 1980, in 2000 residences in the Dusseldorf/Neuss area, another 2000 in Berlin, and an additional 1000 in each location nominated by IPs. Bildschirmtext adaptors were supplied free by TV manufacturers, though participants had to furnish their own color TV sets. In addition they had to pay a monthly rate of DM 5 (about $2), plus, of course, local telephone service charges. Although IPs were permitted to charge for frames, most of the information was supplied at no cost during the trial.

On October 1, 1980, the first external computers were connected to the Bildschirmtext system, enabling subscribers to communicate with the computers of three mail-order firms, a bank and a travel agency. By June 1981, 11 external computers were connected and owners of another 20 had applied to do so.

Complaints from participants in the early stages of the trial centered on predictable grievances: "too much advertising and self-presentation by firms," frame charges levied by IPs without advance warning, and computer breakdowns. One of the interesting aspects of the trial was that the organizers had difficulty attracting the full complement of 2000 participants in Dusseldorf, because they had set out to have a cross section of occupational groups. Not surprisingly, applicants tended to have high income and education levels; unskilled and skilled workers and foremen were poorly represented.

In general, German publishers and other IPs devoted significant sums to preparing information for the Bildschirmtext system; especially heavy costs were incurred by those implementing the software needed to link their computers to the Bildschirmtext centers. According to Ulrich Bottcher, head of the Bildschirmtext Service for Fernmeldetechnisches Zentralamt, "many television set manufacturers have shown less interest in Bildschirmtext than the information providers..." This attitude began to change somewhat after the German Cabinet agreed to permit Bildschirmtext to be used for individual communications (such as electronic mail) and agreement of European telecommunications authorities on common videotext standards in May 1981.

The technical dimensions of Bildschirmtext are quite similar to those of Prestel, with all the limitations of the "tree structure" index and the inability to search by subject, except in the crudest sense. The first weeks of the field trials saw numerous computer hardware failures, culminating in a 22-hour outage of the system on September 25, 1980 when a disk memory failed and an entire day's data was lost. Service then improved, and was deemed of "satisfactory quality" a year later. By fall 1981, more than 5000 subscribers were connected—3000 in Berlin and about 2200 in Dusseldorf/Neuss. By June 1982, the number of frames stored had reached almost 200,000 and daily calls to the two centers were running at the rate of 800 to 1000 for each. About one million calls were placed in the first two years of operation, with an average daily connect time of about 20 minutes.

The Federal Cabinet has authorized commercial Bildschirmtext service beginning in autumn 1983, with subscriber-to-subscriber messages permitted as of that date. Bildschirmtext centers will gradually be established in the principal central and regional telephone exchanges; the Deutsche Bundespost expects to sign one million subscribers by the end of 1986. In November 1981, the Bundespost awarded initial contracts totalling $22.5 million to IBM to supply the central computers, which will be IBM system 4300 and series 1 processors.

From the papers presented by Bildschirmtext spokesmen at international conferences, it appears that the Deutsche Bundespost, undaunted by the cool reception given Prestel in the U.K., is aiming squarely at the home market that the Prestel creators once had in their sights. Cold reality eventually forced the British to shift to the business market. Whether the gateway feature, permitting a wide variety of transaction services in the home, will make any difference in Germany is an open question.

GREECE

In May 1982 the Bank of Thessalia, an international financial institution, announced plans to implement an extensive French Teletel videotext system in Greece. When the service is in full operation, it is expected to involve a network of 4500 terminals, supplied by Telic Alcatel. The system will also use 30 Videopac-400 software packages from Steria and 30 DPS 6 minicomputers manufactured by Cii Honeywell Bull.

A major objective of the plan is to place leased terminals in public locations, such as food stores, gas stations and drug stores, so that they can function as alternative bank branches. Customers will be able to use the service free of charge.

The estimated cost of this videotext project is $10 million. Two central videotext offices will be established in Athens with eight branches in other cities throughout Greece.

HUNGARY

Research on viewdata and teletext systems began in 1978 at Budapest Technical University. A research team at the university conducted the first field trials involving teletext in 1980, with further tests in 1981. The system used color television sets incorporating Mullard/Phillips teletext decoders to receive teletext transmission. It is estimated that the cost of a color TV set equipped with a decoder will be about 30% higher than a standard set. In 1981, the projected date for an experimental teletext service was 1982.

The research team also conducted viewdata experiments. After much investigation, the Swedish computer ABC-80, made by Luxor, was chosen to implement a viewdata system. Beginning in 1982, a closed user group (CUG) will be available to professional organizations since the high price of the decoder makes it more affordable for businesses than for private subscribers. During 1982 also, a decision will be made concerning the exact system and types of information to be offered on a permanent basis.

ITALY

In 1982-1983 the Italian Telephone Operating Company (SIP), authorized by the Minister of Post and Telecommunications, is coordinating a videotext experiment known as Videotel. The purpose of this trial phase is threefold: 1) to determine reactions of IPs and users; 2) to uncover technical difficulties; and 3) to encourage the industry to confront problems and develop solutions prior to the implementation of a full scale public service.

The success of this trial is dependent on the cooperation of the participants who include the Italian PTT (Post and Telecommunications Administration), the SIP, broadcasting companies, and various industries and research institutions. The service may be free to users and IPs while training is taking place during the experimental phase, but tariffs may later be imposed.

The final Italian videotext system will consist of 96 ports, two GEC 4082 computers and a capacity of more than 50,000 pages.

JAPAN

The development of videotext services in Japan has been shaped by the special characteristics of the Japanese language. With its complex mixture of Japanese syllabaries (hirogana and katakana) and as many as 3000 kanji characters, Japanese has always been difficult to reproduce and transmit by mechanical means (see Figures 9.1 and 9.2). This fact is one reason facsimile transmission and the production of low cost fax transceivers have

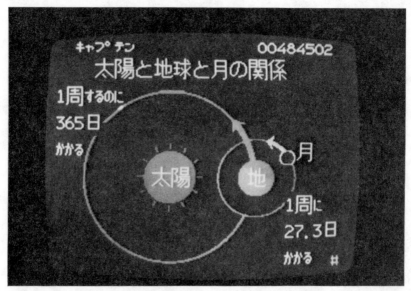

Figure 9.1 The CAPTAIN system in Japan is equipped to handle graphics expertly since they are an integral part of the communication process. Courtesy CAPTAIN.

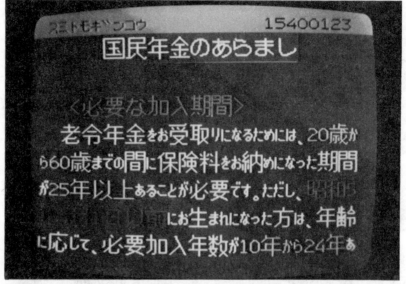

Figure 9.2 The technology of the CAPTAIN system is capable of reproducing and transmitting difficult Japanese characters and symbols. Courtesy CAPTAIN.

advanced so rapidly in Japan. Thus, from the outset, a videotext service in Japan had to be designed with extraordinary capability for handling graphics.

CAPTAIN (Character And Pattern Telephone Access Information Network) was developed jointly by the Ministry of Posts and Telecommunications and by Nippon Telegraph & Telephone (NTT). It uses standard telephone circuits with full duplex transmission lines. Messages are transmitted from center to user terminals at the rate of 3200 bps; those from user to central computer travel at the rate of 75 bps.

The system began experimental service in the Tokyo area on December 25, 1979. In the first phase, lasting until March 1981, 1000 residential users were connected to the CAPTAIN center. At that point a second, more extensive trial began. Five hundred additional terminals were installed in business locations and the data base was augmented by business and economic information.

Among the technical features of CAPTAIN that help distinguish it from other videotext systems around the world are the following:

- use of a bit-plane memory at the user terminal, and sending of frames by a technique known as pattern transmission, in which both characters and graphics are transmitted as dot patterns suitable for display on a screen, according to S. Harashima and M. Kobayashi of NTT;

- storage of information frames in either coded or dot pattern form in the CAPTAIN computer, depending on storage space required. Thus, kanji, kana (Japanese syllabary) and alphanumerics are stored in coded form, while pictorial information is stored in dot patterns. To transmit a frame, coded information is converted into dot pattern images by a character generator at the CAPTAIN center, before transmission to the user;

- use of a redundancy compression technique known as "one-dimensional run-length coding" to form a frame on the screen in no more than 10 seconds; and use of a bit-transparent transmission technique for efficient transmission of dot pattern data; and

- ability to "read" graphics into the system by use of a facsimile terminal or TV camera; the resulting images are digitized automatically, with color added manually. (While these techniques of data compression and transmission might be employed in European and American videotext systems, there is less need to do so there than in Japan, since far more information is required to create a frame in the Japanese language.)

As of early 1982 CAPTAIN served a total of 2000 user terminals; 1200 for residential customers, 500 for business customers, 200 for IPs and 100 for exhibition and system development. One hundred ninety-nine IPs supplied 98,944 initial frames of information, and within the first 15 months had created another 204,310 updated frames. The largest percentage of frames related to amusement and hobbies (20%), followed by: news and weather reports (16%), sports (14%), education and culture (9%), business information (8%) and shopping information (8%).[2]

The pattern of use in the initial phase, however, was even more heavily weighted toward amusement and hobbies. These frames accounted for 47% of all retrieval, followed by 10.6% for news and weather, and 10.3% for education and culture. Among the specific items that were highly popular were games and quizzes, including a verson of "igo" (Japanese Go).

Users in the initial phase of CAPTAIN liked the service, with about half saying they would subscribe when it was offered commercially. Thirty percent said they would use it if the particular information offered was of value, while 20% said they were not interested. As to cost, only 30% of those in the trial were willing to pay more than 3000 yen per month (about $13).

Trial users were most willing to pay for information in the following categories: 1) seat reservations (as with other videotext services, finding out whether airplane seats were available has been a popular use); 2) entertainment; 3) practical everyday information; 4) travel and hotel information; 5) cooking; 6) books; and 7) games.

Based on results from the two trial phases, officials at the Ministry of Posts and Telecommunications and at NTT decided to introduce a commercial videotext service which would begin in 1983 and reach full potential two or three years later. The service is to encompass the following features: 1) interactive information retrieval from a data base; 2) closed user groups and other systems for business applications; 3) home-oriented business transactions; and 4) message switching. The closed business services are seen as necessary to link low cost videotext terminals with online computer systems. At present there are about 5000 such computer systems operating in Japan, and more than 100,000 leased circuits for data communications; both have been increasing at the rate of 35% a year. Nevertheless, since these services will not reach shops, smaller professional businesses and homes, CAPTAIN is seen as a way of providing low cost access to computerized information.

The third category, transaction services, will build on a simple order entry system in use in the second CAPTAIN trial. By linking consumers to third-party computers, CAPTAIN will make possible reservations, catalog shopping and banking on a 24-hour-a-day, seven-day-a-week basis.

The fourth service, message switching, requires a redesign and upgrading of the CAPTAIN system. The intention would be to let subscribers send messages to other subscribers, as in other electronic mail services.

Standardization

The special graphic needs of a Japanese videotext system to store and transmit graphics appear to rule out standardization with other systems around the world in the near future. The CAPTAIN system requires more expensive storage features and character generators than are in use in other countries. Thus, it is hardly likely to serve as a model for these countries. Within Japan the Ministry of Posts and Telecommunications has worked with the Japanese TV network, NHK (Nippon Hoso Kyokai) and other Japanese commercial broadcasters on compatability between CAPTAIN terminals and the prototype teletext adaptors used by broadcasters.

Status of Broadcast Teletext in Japan

Broadcast teletext has been under study and development by Japan's broadcasters for a number of years. NHK (Nippon Hoso Kyokai) has been conducting research at its large research center, NHK Technical Research Laboratories. In February 1976 it published a proposal for a Text Television System, and late in 1978 began broadcasting experimental teletext pages. The NHK system, known as CIBS (Character Information Broadcasting Station), is based on a matrix of dots, with 332 dots per line and 200 lines per frame. As with the CAPTAIN system, this technology requires a substantial amount of memory in the receiver.

The legal groundwork for the commencement of teletext services was cleared by the Ministry of Posts and Telecommunications in March 1982 when it formulated legislation to be presented to the Diet. Teletext services are officially labelled "Television Letter-and-Character Multiplex Broadcasting." In order to prevent monopolization of teletext by existing broadcasters, the legislation was to provide for the leasing of at least some of the time available to an impartial third party institution. Assuming passage by the Diet, the legal authorization for teletext would take effect in 1983.

Economics of Videotext in Japan

Notably absent from published papers dealing with videotext in Japan is any discussion of the cost of the CAPTAIN trial service, not to mention any projection of the investment and operating expenses required for a commercial service. Since more computer power is needed in the CAPTAIN center, and since more expensive terminals are required for user display, it stands to reason that a system like CAPTAIN will be considerably more costly to operate than one like Prestel in the U.K., Bildschirmtext in Germany, or Knight-Ridder's Viewtron in the U.S. How this fact can be reconciled with the apparent unwillingness of most Japanese in the CAPTAIN trial to pay more than $13 a month for the service remains to be seen. Certainly it appears that in Japan, as elsewhere, the economic realities of home information retrieval, rather than the technical problems of building reliable computer systems and workable terminals, pose the real obstacles to development of videotext in the current decade.

Role of Japanese Companies in Videotext Abroad

One additional aspect of Japanese involvement in videotext should be mentioned: the potential role of suppliers of decoders and integrated circuits to the rest of the world. Japanese companies like Sony, Matsushita, NEC, Sharp and Hitachi have demonstrated their ability to mass produce TV sets, video cassette recorders and other items of consumer electronics. Should a mass market begin to develop for teletext or videotext decoders in the U.S. or Europe, there is nothing to stop Japanese companies from jumping in to supply equipment, whatever the peculiar problems of the Japanese domestic market.

NETHERLANDS

Viditel, the one year viewdata trial in operation in the Netherlands, is being conducted by the Netherlands PTT with permission granted by the Dutch government.

The trial system, which uses a GEC 4082 computer with a memory of 384 kilobytes, also has been serving CUGs since July 1979. As of February 1982, 130 independent IPs and about 450 sub-IPs were involved in the trial. Modems were supplied by the PTT to 5000 subscribers who pay normal subscriber charges during the trial as well as any additional fees imposed by the IPs. The IPs participate free of charge, but the PTT requires them to introduce one new user to the system, with equipment and subscription, for every 75 pages of information they supply.

The Viditel trial and research will continue until early 1983 when the Dutch government will reach a decision regarding the implementation of a full viewdata service.

NORWAY

A videotext field trial has been underway in Norway since 1980. The service, known as Teledata, has a page capacity of 4000. As of February 1982, 100 sets were in use and 40 IPs were participating. A government decision is expected in mid-1982 to determine the structure of a full commercial service.

SPAIN

The Spanish Videotext Project can provide information to users on current events, financial statistics, bookings and even home study courses. The system requires the use of the Spanish Packet Transmission Network (RETD), slanted pictorial characters and alphanumeric characters. IPs include newspapers, magazines, schools and banks. Among the services already planned are ready-reference, promotion and message exchange. It is also possible that testing will be conducted for telebanking, teleshopping and electronic telephone listings.

There are three stages in the Spanish Videotext Project. The pilot trial was primarily promotional and ran from February 1980 through March 1981. In the experimental stage a field trial was conducted and involved at least 200 terminals. All of the subscriber equipment was supplied by the Spanish National Telephone Company (CTNE). The third stage is a trial service beginning in mid-1982 and ending in May 1983. Part of this involved using videotext for external communications in conjunction with the World Football Championship in 1982.

At the completion of these stages, a decision will be made by the CTNE regarding the implementation of a Spanish videotext system, the exact range of services to be offered and the technical components that will be required.

SWEDEN

Videotext and teletext services are seen in Sweden as socially important for the disabled, disadvantaged and minority groups. In 1978, when the Commission on New Information Technology was formed to evaluate electronic information systems, it asked the Swedish Broadcasting Corporation (SBC) to serve these populations.

Broadcast teletext, known as "Text-TV," has been in fairly wide use in Sweden since 1979/1980. The system, controlled entirely by the SBC, has a channel capacity of 800 pages. Approximately 100,000 receivers had been installed in homes throughout the country as of February 1982. In mid-1982, a videotext service for business subscribers is planned by the Swedish Telecommunications Administration. "Teledata," the Swedish term for videotext, was not offered to the public as of June 1981. However, there has been great enthusiasm and support for a generally available service.

By 1985, most Swedish television sets will be equipped to receive broadcast teletext. (These sets cost $200 more than conventional TVs.) Between 1985 and 1999 it is possible that all telephone subscribers will receive videotext terminals instead of printed telephone directories.

SWITZERLAND

A Swiss viewdata pilot trial has been in operation since November 1979. It was initiated by the Swiss PTT which selected Standard Telephone and Radio AG (STR) as the general contractor. As of May 1981, subscribers included 86 independent business organizations and 27 PTT departments. The service uses Prestel technology and will continue until the end of 1982.

In 1983, a test service for 2000 subscribers will begin. Its objectives are: to test the reactions of private subscribers; to evaluate the technical aspects; and to find the best means of implementing a three language service (Swiss, German and French). It is hoped that a smooth transition to public service can be made at the completion of the test phase.

NOTES

1. Information in this chapter is based on data provided by a variety of sources, including Communications Studies and Planning International (New York City); *Videotex—Key to the Information Revolution* (Middlesex, UK: Online Conferences Ltd., 1982) and various international videotext-related organizations.

2. *Videotex '81* (Middlesex, UK: Online Conferences Ltd., 1981), p. 118.

10

Conclusions

by Efrem Sigel

EVOLUTION OF VIDEOTEXT

For more than 500 years print on paper has dominated intellectual life in the Western world. The invention of moveable type and the printing press shook the established order of crown and clergy, breaking the Church's monopoly on knowledge and monarchical control over political expression. With an efficient, low cost means of disseminating knowledge, science and technology received an indispensable stimulus: scientific progress depends heavily on communication, and the printing press became the instrument of that communication.

Only in the last one hundred years have other media developed to augment, but not supplant, the role of print. The phonograph, the radio, the motion picture, the television were all developments of the last 25 years of the 19th century, or the first 25 years of the new century. Taken together they have revolutionized popular culture, leisure time and entertainment; their influence on science, scholarship and education is certainly less direct, though in the end it may prove to be fundamental.

In the last 30 years, however, has come the rise of a new information machine of awesome power: the computer. Many of us have difficulty conceiving of computers as communications media, because our perception of them is heavily influenced by their early role as giant bookkeeping-accounting-calculating machines. The true power of the computer has become evident, however, in interactive time-sharing systems that permit thousands of users simultaneously to retrieve information from a large data base or data bank. When such a system is applied to the information we are accustomed to receiving in printed form, i.e., through newspapers, magazines, scientific journals, business newsletters or government statistical reports, then a dramatic transformation is possible in how information is gathered, weighed, edited, published and consumed. Indeed, the very definition of "publish" is subject to reinterpretation. Computer-based information systems allow each reader to define his own publication, assembling information from a variety of sources, accepting some, discarding others and combining them with his own interpretation.

Videotext is one manifestation of this new world of communications. But despite the claims of its devotees, the world is unknown, the technology unproved and the demand for it largely non-existent. In the United States alone, over $30 billion is spent annually to support the production of printed publications. The comparable figure for publications received electronically, i.e., over a printer or video display screen, is less than $1 billion. And the amount spent for information in the particular format of videotext—i.e., in a page-by-page format featuring seven or eight colors and capable of display on an adapted television receiver—is probably less than $10 million.

As we have seen in Chapter 3, most information that is delivered electronically goes to business and professional customers, not consumers in their homes. No one knows if the latter want or can afford such services. On the evidence to date, not many of them do. In the United Kingdom, the Prestel service had barely 30,000 customers by the end of 1983; only four years earlier, its proponents had talked ambitiously of reaching 250,000 by this date. Prestel was forced to trim its staff, shut down regional computers, shift from a consumer to business emphasis, and otherwise act to close a horrendous gap between revenue and outlay. The service has cost British Telecom millions of pounds since its inception.

Prestel may be the most dramatic example of videotext's shortcomings, but it is far from the only one. In France, long delays preceded the launching of the PTT's experimental service, Teletel, in July 1981. Despite extravagant funding from French governmental authorities, there was no reason to think French consumers would react any more positively than their British counterparts to the idea of information delivered through a video terminal. In Holland, the PTT's Viditel service has attracted few residential customers, and Dutch publishers talk freely, if privately, about their disappointment at its reception.

Nor has experience in the U.S. been any different. Two time-sharing services aimed at the home market, The Source and CompuServe, have struggled with consumer indifference. The Source (owned by Reader's Digest and Control Data, which invested in it in 1983) had fewer than 50,000 subscribers in 1983. Although it had emphasized the consumer market, the company discovered to its astonishment that many of its customers were actually business organizations.

Time Inc., Knight-Ridder, CBS and AT&T are among the many large publishing and communications companies investing millions of dollars in testing a consumer videotext market. But these investments, like those of Reader's Digest or H&R Block (owner of CompuServe), can be seen as largely defensive. Reader's Digest derives more than $1 billion in revenue from selling printed magazines and books to consumers around the world. If there is any likelihood that print will some day yield to electronics, isn't it prudent for the Digest to hedge its bets? For that huge publisher, spending a couple of million dollars on a venture like The Source is comparable to a homeowner's outlay of $500 annually for fire and theft insurance. If nothing happens to his house he's happy to spend the money. In the same way, if nothing happens to disturb the Digest's profits from magazine circulation and book sales, its losses from The Source will be money well spent.

The fundamental problem with videotext for consumers is a misapprehension about why individuals read newspapers, magazines and books. Just because these publications contain news and information does not mean that the average reader avidly turns to their pages to retrieve the latest facts and to put them to work in his daily life. In fact, any reading at home is first and foremost a recreational activity, a pastime, and only secondarily is it a purposeful hunt for new information. No one would read the daily paper, *Newsweek* magazine or a nonfiction book like *Freedom at Midnight* unless they conveyed information in an entertaining manner. But delivering information over a terminal is anything but entertaining. Screens are meant for retrieving a desired fact or number and then going on to something else. They do not encourage the reader to linger over his favorite data base, or to share an amusing anecdote with spouse or family. They are ideal for transactions, whether it is one involving banking, shopping or information. A banking transaction involves debits or credits; it is not an end in itself, but the necessary accompaniment to getting paid, or to paying someone else. A shopping transaction involves ordering a good or service; this too is a means of obtaining what is wanted, not a value for its own sake. In the same way, an information transaction involves keying in a new fact or retrieving an existing one. It too is an aspect of a wider process, rather than an activity that many people engage in to pass time.

Need for Information

Recognizing this feature of information retrieval is an important clue to knowing just when a videotext or online service makes sense. When I use the Paris telephone directory or R.R. Bowker's *Books in Print* or *Who's*

Who to find a telephone number, to check the spelling of an author's name or the year in which Lord Mountbatten was born, the item of information is to be put to immediate use. It is grist for some sort of transaction: a phone call I will make, a book I will order, or a footnote I will add to a paper I am writing. In many such transactions, speed is of the essence. Take investing—when an investor looks up the recent history of a company in a reporting service from *Moody's* or *Standard & Poor's*, it is with a very single-minded purpose: do I or do I not buy (sell) shares in such a company? If retrieving the desired information through a terminal speeds up the process, allows one to make a decision quicker, and buy or sell immediately, then the cost of getting the information in that manner is insignificant. The real cost is the cost of not having the information when it is needed.

Farmers know, to their chagrin, the cost of not having information on markets on a timely basis. If the price of wheat has dropped 10 cents a bushel in the past hour and the farmer hopes that day to sell 50,000 bushels, a few dollars to obtain the latest price is the wisest expenditure he can make. It's no accident then, that news wires for farmers are booming and that the interactive retrieval of commodity price information is already well established. Such systems get their start with large brokers, traders and commercial farmers, but once they exist, no one in the market can afford to be without them, unless he is willing to do business at a severe handicap. Whether a stock broker is with the largest firm, Merrill Lynch, or a small local company, the online stock quote service is a necessity, in the same way that a businessman needs a telephone whether he works for General Motors in Detroit or AAA Auto Parts in New Rochelle, NY.

Information transactions—the process of obtaining facts to accomplish some goal—take place in both business and residential settings. What is different is the need for speed, and the economic magnitude of the decision. A purchasing manager in a manufacturing company must buy raw materials continuously, or the assembly line will shut down and his company will be out of business. A consumer who needs new furniture can generally take his time (even if he's in a hurry, the furniture supplier will make him take his time). Investing is another example of the different economic imperatives. A consumer with a few thousand dollars to invest will forsake perhaps $150 per year if the money sits in a savings account at low interest, instead of a certificate of deposit earning a higher rate. A company with tens of millions of dollars in cash to invest daily, however, would be giving up more than $50,000 a year by not getting the best return on its money. The example can be repeated many times over: the payoffs for having and using information on time are far greater in the business and professional world than in the world of residential consumers.

VIDEOTEXT, BROADCASTERS AND THE TV SET

Until the decade of the 1970s, broadcasters the world over virtually controlled the use of the home TV set. There was no programming available except what was transmitted over-the-air, no reason to have a set except to receive such programming. Cable television, pay TV, video games, video cassette recorders, video disc players and videotext have all contributed to a severing of this tight bond between the set owner and the broadcaster. At any given moment in a home in the U.S., what appears on the screen can now come from dozens, hundreds, even thousands of sources: a pay TV service, a regular cable program, a video game cartridge, a personal computer program or a teletext transmission.

Most of this programming consists of entertainment. The pay TV networks that reached 17 million homes by late 1983 grew to prominence by a steady diet of Hollywood films—films that were uninterrupted by commercials. Video recorders are used primarily to tape programs off the air, secondarily to play back movies. Video games are light entertainment with an occasional instructional program thrown in.

Videotext, along with the personal computer, is one of the few new electronic technologies whose application is devoted to information, current awareness and education. While this sets it apart from other media, it also indicates the problems of consumer acceptance. In the home, television is synonymous with light entertainment, with passing the time. If the audience for documentaries, or for cultural programs aired on the Public Broadcasting Service (PBS) stations, or the Sunday interview shows is any guide, the number of people interested in serious material is but a fraction of the total who watch TV.

Not only does a videotext display suffer from this built-in propensity of viewers to watch TV for pleasure, but it even has difficulty competing with serious TV programs. A videotext screen is not an audiovisual program, but a display of text. It has no still or moving pictures, no sound, no drama, no emotional content. Particularly in the evening, when the average viewer is not in the mood for sustained education or information, the videotext display may be a very poor last in the competition for his time.

There are several caveats to this gloomy prognosis. People will take information in small doses on TV—many broadcasters in the U.S. air 30 seconds of news highlights every hour, in between the regular programs. In addition, broadcasters can offer a teletext service as a way of satisfying those who need up-to-date information without disturbing regular programming. As the BBC's pioneer in teletext, Colin McIntyre, points out, teletext is broadcasting. In a world of increasing competition for the TV set, a broadcast teletext service is a way for the TV station to stake its claim on viewer loyalty. Teletext news and information can serve a number of different constituencies, none of them large by itself, but perhaps totalling a significant minority of the viewing public. This minority includes:

- those who watch little regular TV but want quick updates on what's going on;

- those whose business or profession demands staying in touch; and

- the deaf or hard of hearing, who can only watch programs with captions.

By reaching out to these groups who are not regular customers, the broadcaster can use teletext to expand his audience, and to do a form of targeting of information not possible with normal broadcast programs. Of course, there is a real danger to the broadcaster in promoting teletext: the possibility that regular TV watchers will switch on their decoders and turn off "Monday Night Football" or "Dallas." If this happens, broadcast audiences will decline, and so will advertising revenues. In principle, however, teletext is one of the few ways—other than raising prices—that a broadcaster can actually increase revenues. Unlike a magazine or newspaper publisher, the broadcaster cannot expand air time to meet demand; the number of hours in the day is fixed. Putting information on the vertical blanking interval (VBI), and either charging viewers for that information or charging advertisers to sponsor it, is, for the broadcaster, the same as a print publisher adding a new section to his daily paper.

In Europe, where broadcasting is supported by government funding and need not respond as directly to market pressures, teletext can be viewed as a means of enhanced public service. The BBC is fond of pointing out that the cost of supporting CEEFAX works out to only a couple of pennies per household per year, out of an annual license fee that totals about £46 for color, slightly less for black and white. (The counter-argument, of course, would be that with teletext receivers in only about 650,000 British homes, 20 million license holders are paying for a service that only 3.25% of them so far have evinced any interest in obtaining.)

TECHNICAL STANDARDS AND VIDEOTEXT

A debate over technical standards has dominated the early years of videotext, often to the exclusion of more fundamental issues. Once the British, French and Canadians had each adopted incompatible national systems, the race was on to sell technology to the rest of the world. The big prize has been the United States, but the battle has also raged in Europe (Germany, Italy, Belgium), Australia and Latin America (Venezuela, Brazil, Mexico).

Standards are necessary in many industries where customers need to communicate using compatible equipment. The telephone and telecommunications industry is an obvious example. Since viewdata systems were developed by centralized, government-owned PTTs, and are meant to operate over the public telephone network, entering the European market could only be accomplished by persuading a government-owned PTT to adopt a given technical standard. Broadcasting is another industry where customers need common equipment if they are to receive transmissions from radio and TV stations; this is true whether the dominant form of broadcasting is commercial stations, as in North America, or public authorities, as in Europe.

Yet the development of videotext has also coincided with a worldwide trend toward deregulation of both telephone telecommunications and broadcasting. In the U.S. the 1970s has seen the burgeoning of a private interconnect industry offering equipment in competition with the Bell System and telecommunications services in competition with AT&T Long Lines. In the U.K. British Telecom has been split off from the British Post Office and subjected to certain competitive forces for the first time in history.

Similar deregulation is underway in broadcasting. In the U.S. cable TV has been freed of rules in order to compete with over-the-air broadcasting. In the U.K. a second commercial channel will soon be operating, giving commercial broadcasters two channels to the two channels controlled by the BBC. In France the legal monopoly on broadcasting long enjoyed by the government-owned Telediffusion de France is also under attack. All over Europe, cable TV, pay TV and satellite transmission are in various stages of study or implementation, further eroding the power of the public authorities. The boom in video cassette recorder sales in Europe, and the attending popularity of renting films on cassette, attest to the public's appetite for programming not under the control of a central broadcasting office.

In the midst of this turmoil, the push for uniform teletext and viewdata standards is a bit of an anomaly. It harkens back to an earlier era of careful control over who had access to the public airwaves, and for what purpose. In European countries like Britain, France and Germany, public broadcasting organizations will set the rules for teletext, while government-run telecommunications authorities will dominate whatever viewdata services exist. But in the U.S. this same pattern will not prevail. The decision of the FCC in October 1981 was testimony to this fact. By freeing any broadcaster to use whatever teletext system he desires, the FCC stated in unmistakable terms that it would not get involved in determining either technical standards, or the wisdom of offering a teletext service.

In the North American environment, viewdata is likely to follow a similar, perhaps even more fragmented path. Viewdata services over telephone lines are just another variant of computerized information retrieval services, such as are offered by Lockheed's Dialog, by Mead, by Dow Jones and by Bibliographic Retrieval Services. These suppliers compete in the marketplace for customers, and any standardization of data transmission or display is as a result of voluntary agreement, not government fiat. The new element in this environment is the decision of AT&T to be actively involved in information retrieval. The Bell System has long set de facto North American standards for telephone equipment and service. Since it can single-handedly create a market for videotext terminals, its wishes will have considerable sway in the marketplace.

Evolution of Technology and Effect on Standards

Because the decade of the 1980s promises to be a fertile period for telecommunications, the early years of that decade may be exactly the wrong time to settle on technical standards for videotext, or any other communications medium. In a few short years the alphamosaic displays of Prestel and Antiope have given way to the richer, more advanced system known as Telidon. AT&T's Presentation Level Protocol for videotext promises still more technically advanced display of text and graphics. Nor is this going to be the end. All the major systems have demonstrated techniques for sending full color, still photographs. Interconnections with microcomputers are becoming available that permit ready printout of viewdata frames, as well as easier indexing and retrieval of specific items of information contained in those frames. (As of October 1981, Prestel was making available discs that made possible the linking of an Apple II with the Prestel data base.) As the cost of memory drops, terminals will enter the market that feature storage of many hundreds, even thousands of viewdata frames by the user.

As long as system suppliers maintain their commitment to make devices "upward compatible," (meaning that earlier terminals will still be able to display some version of more sophisticated systems), technical progress can continue without rendering obsolete earlier equipment. The point must be made, however, that very few videotext terminals are installed in commercial quantities around the world. Counting every single demonstration project in every country, plus the few commercial services, the total of teletext decoders was perhaps two million by the end of 1983—with more than half of them in Britain alone. The number of viewdata terminals was under 50,000, again with half of them in the U.K. These numbers can hardly justify freezing technical standards in order to protect existing users. Indeed, given the rapid development of the technology and the still-rudimentary stage of its acceptance, the opposite argument carries more weight. To base technical standards on current equipment penalizes the 99% of homes and businesses that are not now videotext users, but that might be if the systems were more technically advanced, more versatile, and easier to operate.

RELATIONSHIP BETWEEN VIDEOTEXT AND OTHER COMMUNICATIONS TECHNOLOGIES

Neither teletext nor viewdata exists in isolation; they are available at the same time as a host of other technologies for transmitting and displaying information. It may be helpful to summarize the status of some of these alternatives in both the professional and residential markets.

Business/Professional Markets

The technologies that are most competitive with videotext in the business and professional market are those that use telecommunications to move information from one location to another, or to retrieve it from a remote computer data bank. These include:

Online Retrieval Services. By the end of 1983, the principal U.S. distributors of online data bases, including Dialog Information Services, Bibliographic Retrieval Services, Dow Jones, Reuters, and McGraw-Hill, had a total of 550,000 customers. The advantage of these services compared to viewdata is that they permit much more extensive indexing, and much more precise retrieval of desired information. Instead of locating only the frame that has a desired fact, or instead of a cumbersome frame-by-frame search, as with viewdata, the online data base permits location of a key word, phrase or name that is being sought. Thus, it's an inherently more flexible, if more expensive, medium.

Personal Computers. The personal computer has had a dramatic impact on the business world in the past three years, and as its popularity has grown, its effect on the nascent videotext market will be decisive. In 1983, an estimated 1.6 million personal computers (costing $2000 and up) were sold in the U.S., up from 900,000 in 1982 and 440,000 in 1981. Expenditures on personal computer hardware and software reached an estimated $8.5 billion in the U.S. in 1983.

Because the personal computer can be used to access online data bases in a conventional ASCII format (black and white only, in an 80 character by 25-line display), their penetration has given a great boost to services like Dow Jones News/Retrieval and CompuServe. With personal computer manufacturers like IBM, Apple, Hewlett-Packard, and Digital Equipment Corp. all viewing the personal computer as central to office automation and electronic business communication, the possibilities for installing separate videotext services in the corporate world would appear to have greatly diminished—unless these services can adapt to the personal computer as the preferred retrieval and display terminal.

Communicating Word Processors. A small computer programmed to edit and rearrange text rather than to perform computations, the word processor underwent a boom in sales and usage in the early 1980s. When communications capability is added, the word processor becomes a key element in an electronic mail system, and a far more versatile terminal than a simple videotext device. Sales of personal computers, however, appear to be cutting into the dedicated word processor market.

Facsimile Transceivers. High-speed fax units, capable of sending an 8½ x 11-inch page of text in under a minute, are becoming far more common in the business world. Facsimile, of course, provides a paper copy of whatever is transmitted (unlike videotext), and is ideal for messages containing graphics as well as text.

Optical (Laser) Video Discs. The laser disc offers possibilities both for audiovisual programming, as in a conventional videotaped training program, and for information storage and retrieval. Used as a data storage device, the laser disc can hold the equivalent of 3200 300-page books. Where a large, fairly static data base of information must be available for look-up by many individual users, it makes economic sense to place such a data base on a video disc and make copies widely available.

Video Conferencing Terminals. Communications satellites now available in North America and soon to be proliferating in Europe, offer businessmen a communications channel for face-to-face discussion. The video teleconference can take place using either large-screen video projectors (expensive, but practical when large groups are involved, as in medical meetings, shareholder meetings or presentations to widely scattered dealers and customers) or on a small-screen terminal like AT&T's Picturephone.

Consumer Markets

The above technologies are only some of the ways of moving information from one place to another as alternatives to videotext. In the consumer market, the alternatives are more oriented toward entertainment, as can be seen from the following examples:

Video Cassette Recorders. The ½-inch VCR is fast becoming a ubiquitous accessory to the television set, both for recording programs off-air so they can be seen at another time, and for playing back prerecorded movies that are bought or rented. In Britain, where the VCR became available at about the same time as the teletext decoder, the comparative popularity of the VCR is undeniable. By the end of 1981 there were an estimated 800,000 to one million VCRs in Britain, compared to only 250,000 to 300,000 teletext decoders.

Video Games. The hardware for playing video games costs $100 to $200, and individual game cartridges retail for about $20 to $30. According to the 1982 Consumer Electronics Annual Review published by the Electronic Industries Association, sales of home video games and cartridges hit the $1 billion mark in 1981. Industry sources expect it to increase by another 75% in 1982.

Home Computers. From sales of 2 million units in 1982, home computer shipments have soared to perhaps 4 million to 5 million in 1983, despite losses at major manufacturers like Texas Instruments and Atari. Most such devices, costing $200 and under, are used for playing games or to introduce kids to the computer. But adding an inexpensive modem means the home computer can be used to communicate with online data bases, thus making it potent competition for a dedicated videotext terminal. IBM's PCjr. at $700 is, after all, a much more versatile machine than AT&T's videotext terminal at $900.

Cable and Pay Television. By the end of 1983 some 31 million homes in the U.S. will have cable; at least half of these will be taking a pay TV channel. Cable is being unshackled in Britain and several other European countries; it is already far along in Holland. Cable may offer the lowest cost way of getting videotext into the home, since the cost of using a spare channel is nearly free. On the other hand, the more programming that is available on existing channels, the harder time a videotext information service will have in attracting consumer attention.

CONCLUSIONS

The range of complementary and competing services to videotext only complicates the prognosis for this fascinating, but undeveloped technology. Videotext in its early years has suffered from being the captive of three different types of organizations: the government bureaucracy, the telephone company (whether private or government-owned) and the broadcaster. While each has its reasons for spurring (or retarding) the growth of interactive information retrieval, none is skilled at the real essence of videotext: the gathering, writing, editing and marketing of textual information. This is the function of a publisher, not a telecommunications company or a broadcaster. In the end, videotext will stand or fall as a publishing medium. The market is as varied as the market for many thousands of printed publications—and every bit as difficult to understand. How the market for videotext will develop is not easy to predict, although preceding chapters have certainly indicated one point of view: that business, not consumer applications will predominate; that fact retrieval, not the reading of large amounts of text will be the key application. Beyond this prediction the timing and shape of videotext services are nearly impossible to determine. Videotext will certainly come more slowly than its boosters have predicted. Given the nearly irresistible appeal of the technology, however, it is bound to come in some form.

Appendix:
Organizations Involved with Videotext

ADDISON-WESLEY PUB. CO.
South St.
Reading, MA 01867
(IP)

AEL MICROTEL LTD.
Business Information Systems
4664 Lougheed Highway
Burnaby, B.C., Alberta, Canada
(TA)

**ALBERTA GOVERNMENT
TELEPHONE**
10020 100 St.
Edmonton, Alberta, Canada
(TA)

**AMERICAN TELEPHONE &
TELEGRAPH (AT&T)**
195 Broadway
New York, NY 10007
(IP, SO, EP, TA)

**AMERICAN TELEVISION &
COMMUNICATIONS CORP.**
160 Inverness Dr. W.
Englewood, CO 80112
(CS)

APPLE COMPUTER INC.
10260 Bandley Dr.
Cupertino, CA 95014
(EP)

AREGON VIEWDATA
2777 Summer St.
Stamford, CT 06905
(O)

**ARETE PUBLISHING CO.,
INC.**
Princeton Forrestal Ctr.
100 College Rd. E.
Princeton, NJ 08540
(IP)

**ASHAHI NATIONAL BROAD-
CASTING**
6-4-10 Roppongi
Minato-ku, Tokyo, 106, Japan
(TV)

ASSOCIATED PRESS
50 Rockefeller Plaza
New York, NY 10020
(IP)

**AT&T LONG LINES
(BELL SYSTEM)**
Bedminster, NJ 07921
(TA)

AVS INTEXT LTD.
145 Oxford St.
London W1R 1TB, England
(IP)

**Key: CS—Cable System; EP—Equipment Provider; IP—Information
Provider; O—Other; SO—System Operator; TA—Telecommunications
Authority; TV—Television Station.**

BANK OF AMERICA
Bank of America Ctr.
PO Box 37000
San Francisco, CA 94137
(IP, SO)

BARCO ELECTRONIC NV
TH Sevenslaan 1.6
8500 Kortrijk, Belgium
(EP)

**BARIC COMPUTING
SERVICES, LTD.**
International Computers Ltd.
Forest Rd.
Feltham, Middlesex, England
(IP)

BELL CANADA
Project Vista
25 Eddy St.
Hull, Quebec, Canada J8Y 6N4
(EP,IP,TA)

**BELL-NORTHERN
RESEARCH LTD.**
PO Box 3511, Station C
Ottawa, Ontario, Canada
K1Y 4H7
(EP)

**BELO INFORMATION
SYSTEMS**
6350 LBJ Freeway, Suite 179
Dallas, TX 75240
(IP)

BILDSCHIRMTEXT
Deutsche Bundespost
Postfach 80 01
5300 Bonn 1
West Germany
(TA)

**BONNEVILLE INTER-
NATIONAL CORP.**
36 S. State St.
Salt Lake City, UT 84111
(TV)

**BRITISH BROADCASTING
CORP.**
Broadcasting House
London W1A 1AA England
(TV)

**BRITISH COLUMBIA
TELEPHONE CO.**
3777 Kingsway
Burnaby, Vancouver, Canada
(TA)

**BRITISH ELECTRONICS
INDUSTRY INFORMATION**
Leicester House
8 Leicester St.
London WC2, England
(O)

**BRITISH RADIO EQUIPMENT
MANUFACTURERS'
ASSOCIATION (BREMA)**
Twentieth Century House
31 Soho Sq.
London W1V 5DG, England
(O)

Key: CS—Cable System; EP—Equipment Provider; IP—Information Provider; O—Other; SO—System Operator; TA—Telecommunications Authority; TV—Television Station.

BRITISH TELECOM
OLC 3.1
Broad St. South
55 Old Broad St.
London EC2M 1RX, England
(TA)

**BRITISH VIDEOTEX &
TELETEXT**
c/o Logica Inc.
666 Third Ave.
New York, NY 10017
(O)

BUTLER COX & PARTNERS
Morley House
26-30 Holborn Viaduct
London EC1A 2 BP, England
(O)

**CANADIAN BROADCASTING
CORP.**
PO Box 8478
Ottawa, Ontario, Canada
K1G 3J5
(TV)

CAP-CPP
14 Great James St.
London WC1, England
(O)

CBS INC.
51 W. 52 St.
New York, NY 10019
(IP, TV)

**CCETT (Centre Commun
d'Etudes de Télévision et Télécommunications)**
PTT-TDF
35 Rennes, France
(TA)

**CCITT (International Telegraph
& Telephone Consultative Com-
mittee)**
International Telecommunication
Union
Place des Nations
CH-1211 Geneva 20
Switzerland
(O)

**CENTRE NATIONAL
d'ETUDES DES TÉLÉCOM-
MUNICATIONS (CNET)**
38-40 rue du Général-Leclerc,
F-92131
Issy-les-Moulineaux, France
(TA)

CHERRY LEISURE
387 High Rd.
London NW10, England
(EP)

CHICAGO PUBLIC LIBRARY
425 N. Michigan Ave.
Chicago, IL 60611
(IP)

CII HONEYWELL BULL
94 Avenue Gambetta
75960 Paris Cedex 20, France
(EP)

**Key: CS—Cable System; EP—Equipment Provider; IP—Information
Provider; O—Other; SO—System Operator; TA—Telecommunications
Authority; TV—Television Station.**

CIT ALCATEL
10 bis rue Louis Lormand
F-78320 La Verriere, France
(EP)

COMMODORE BUSINESS MACHINES, LTD.
3330 Scott Blvd.
Santa Clara, CA 95050
(EP)

COMMUNICATIONS STUDIES AND PLANNING INTERNATIONAL
90 Park Ave.
New York, NY 10016
(O)

COMPUSERVE INFORMATION SERVICE
5000 Arlington Centre Blvd.
Columbus, OH 43220
(IP)

COMPUTEX SYSTEMS LTD.
41 Gloucester Pl.
London WI, England
(EP)

CONSUMERS' ASSOCIATION
14 Buckingham St.
London WC2N 6DS, England
(IP)

CONSUMERS UNION OF THE UNITED STATES
256 Washington St.
Mount Vernon, NY 10550
(IP)

CONTINENTAL TELEPHONE CORP.
245 Perimeter Center Pkwy.
Atlanta, GA 30346
(TA)

COX CABLE COMMUNICATIONS, INC.
219 Perimeter Center Pkwy.
Atlanta, GA 30346
(CS)

CTV TELEVISION NETWORK
42 Charles St. E.
Toronto, Ontario, Canada
M4Y 1T4
(TV)

DECCA RADIO & TELEVISION
Neachalls La.
Willenhall, Wolverhampton, England
(EP)

DEPARTMENT OF COMMUNICATIONS, GOVERNMENT OF CANADA
300 Slater St.
Ottawa, Ontario, Canada
K1A OC8
(TA)

D.E.R.
Apex House
Twickenham Rd.
Feltham, Middlesex, England
(EP)

Key: CS—Cable System; EP—Equipment Provider; IP—Information Provider; O—Other; SO—System Operator; TA—Telecommunications Authority; TV—Television Station.

DIGITAL BROADCASTING CO.
1600 Anderson Rd.
McLean, VA 22102
(SO)

DIGITAL EQUIPMENT CORP.
129 Parker St.
Maynard, MA 01754
(EP)

DIRECTION GENERALE DES TELECOMMUNICATIONS
Direction des Affaires Commerciales et Télématiques
20 rue Las Cases
75007 Paris, France
(TA)

DOMINION DIRECTORY CO. LTD.
Burnaby, B.C., Canada
(IP)

DOW JONES & CO. INC.
22 Cortlandt St.
New York, NY 10007
(IP)

ELECTROHOME LTD. VIDEOTEX MARKETING
809 Wellington St. N.
Kitchener, Ontario, Canada
N2G 4J6
(EP)

ELECTRONIC INDUSTRIES ASSOCIATION
2001 Eye St. NW
Washington, DC 20006
(O)

EXCHANGE TELEGRAPH
Extel House, East Harding St.
London EC4, England
(IP)

FEDERAL COMMUNICATIONS COMMISSION
1919 M St. NW
Washington, DC 20554
(TA)

FERNMELDETECHNISCHES ZENTRALAMT
Referat Datel Services
PO Box 5000
D-6100 Darmstadt
West Germany
(EP)

FIELD ENTERPRISES
401 North Wabash Ave.
Chicago, IL 60611
(IP)

THE FINANCIAL TIMES BUSINESS INFORMATION LTD.
Bracken House
10 Cannon St.
London EC4P 4BY, England
(IP)

FINTEL
102 Clerkenwell Rd.
London EC1M 5SA, England
(IP)

Key: CS—Cable System; EP—Equipment Provider; IP—Information Provider; O—Other; SO—System Operator; TA—Telecommunications Authority; TV—Television Station.

FIRST BANK SYSTEMS INC.
PO Box 422
Minneapolis, MN 55480
(IP, SO)

F.P. PUBLICATIONS LTD.
444 Royal Trust Tower
Toronto, Ontario, Canada
(IP)

GANDALF TECHNOLOGIES INC.
Gandalf Plaza
9 Slack Rd.
Nepean, Ontario, Canada
K2G OB7
(O)

GEC RADIO & TELEVISION
Langley Park
Slough SL3 6DP, England
(EP)

GENERAL ELECTRIC CO. (GEC)
1 Stanhope Gate
London W1, England
(EP)

GENERAL INSTRUMENT CORP.
1775 Broadway
New York, NY 10019
(EP)

GENERAL TELEPHONE & ELECTRONICS (GTE)
1 Stamford Forum
Stamford, CT 06904
(EP, SO, TA)

THE GENESYS GROUP
880 Lady Ellen Pl., Suite 207
Ottawa, Ontario, Canada
K1Z 5L9
(O)

GRANADA TV RENTAL LTD.
Ampthill Rd.
Bedford MK42 9QQ, England
(EP)

GUINNESS SUPERLATIVES
2 Cecil Ct.
London Rd.
Enfield EN2 6DJ, England
(IP)

HEMTON CORP.
1760 Courtwood Cres.
Ottawa, Ontario, Canada
K2C 3L3
(O)

HONEYWELL INC.
200 Smith St.
Waltham, MA 02154
(EP)

IBM CORP.
1133 Westchester Ave.
White Plains, NY 10604
(EP)

Key: CS—Cable System; EP—Equipment Provider; IP—Information Provider; O—Other; SO—System Operator; TA—Telecommunications Authority; TV—Television Station.

**INDEPENDENT BROAD-
CASTING AUTHORITY (IBA)**
70 Brompton Rd.
London SW3 1EY, England
(TV)

INFOMART LTD.
164 Merton St.
Toronto, Ontario, Canada
M4S 3A8
(IP, SO)

**ITT CONSUMER PRODUCTS
(UK) LTD.**
Maidstone Rd., Foots Cray
Sidcup, Kent, England
(EP)

KCET-TV
4400 Sunset Dr.
Los Angeles, CA 90027
(TV)

**KIRBY LESTER ELEC-
TRONICS**
Osborne Industrial Estate
Waddington St.
Oldham OL9 6QQ, England
(EP)

KMOX-TV
1 Memorial Dr.
St. Louis, MO 63102
(TV)

KNBC-TV
3000 W. Alameda
Burbank, CA 91523
(TV)

**KNIGHT-RIDDER NEWS-
PAPERS INC.**
One Herald Plaza
Miami, FL 33101
(IP, SO)

KNXT-TV
6121 Sunset Blvd.
Los Angeles, CA 90028
(TV)

KPIX-TV
2655 Van Ness Ave.
San Francisco, CA 94109
(TV)

KSL-TV
145 Social Hall Ave.
Salt Lake City, UT 84111
(TV)

LABGEAR LTD.
Abbey Walk
Cambridge CB1 2RQ, England
(EP)

**LINK RESOURCES CORP.
(Subsidiary of International Data
Corp.)**
215 Park Ave. S.
New York, NY 10003
(O)

**LOCKHEED INFORMATION
SYSTEMS**
3460 Hillview Ave.
Palo Alto, CA 94304
(SO)

**Key: CS—Cable System; EP—Equipment Provider; IP—Information
Provider; O—Other; SO—System Operator; TA—Telecommunications
Authority; TV—Television Station.**

LOGICA LTD.
64 Newman St.
London W1A 4SE, England
(O)

LONDON STOCK EXCHANGE
London EC2N 1HP, England
(IP)

**MACMILLAN PUBLISHING
CO. INC.**
866 Third Ave.
New York, NY 10022
(IP)

MANHATTAN CABLE TV
120 E. 23 St.
New York, NY 10010
(CS)

**MANITOBA TELEPHONE
SYSTEM**
PO Box 6666
Winnipeg, Manitoba, Canada
R3C 3V6
(TA)

**MATRA TELECOMMUNI-
CATIONS**
Division Internationale
Immeuble International
2 rue Stephenson Rez de Dalle
78181 Saint Quentin en Yvelines
France
(EP)

McGRAW-HILL INC.
1221 Ave. of the Americas
New York, NY 10020
(IP)

MEAD DATA CENTRAL
1828 L St. NW
Suite 803
Washington, DC 20036
(IP)

MERRILL LYNCH & CO. INC.
165 Broadway
New York, NY 10006
(IP, O)

**MICRO TV
(Subsidiary of Radio Broadcast-
ing Co.)**
3600 Conshohocken Ave.
Philadelphia, PA 19131
(TV)

**MILLS & ALLEN COMMUNI-
CATIONS LTD.**
1-4 Langley Ct.
Long Acre, London WC2 9JY
England
(IP)

**MINISTRY OF POSTS AND
TELECOMMUNICATIONS**
20 Avenue de Segur
75700 Paris, France
(TA)

**Key: CS—Cable System; EP—Equipment Provider; IP—Information
Provider; O—Other; SO—System Operator; TA—Telecommunications
Authority; TV—Television Station.**

MITEL CORP.
PO Box 13089
Kanata, Ontario, Canada
K2K 1X3
(EP)

MULLARD LTD.
Millbrook Ind. Est.
Southampton
Hants SO9 7BH, England
(EP)

**NABU MANUFACTURING
CORP.**
485 Richmond Rd.
Ottawa, Ontario, Canada
K2A 3Z2
(EP)

**NATIONAL ASSOCIATION
OF BROADCASTERS**
1771 N St. NW
Washington, DC 20036
(O)

**NATIONAL CABLE TELE-
VISION ASSOCIATION**
918 16 St. NW
Washington, DC 20036
(O)

NEW YORK TIMES CO.
229 W. 43 St.
New York, NY 10036
(IP)

**NIPPON HOSO KYOKAI
(NHK)**
2-2-1 Jin-nan
Shibuya-ku, Tokyo, 150 Japan
(TV)

**NIPPON TELEGRAPH &
TELEPHONE PUBLIC CORP.**
1-1-6, Uchisaiwai-Cho 1-Chome
Chiyoda-Ku
Tokyo 100, Japan
(TA)

NORPAK LTD.
10 Hearst Way
Kanata, Ontario, Canada
K2L 2P4
(EP)

**NORTHERN TELECOM
CANADA LTD.**
304 The East Mall
Islington, Ontario, Canada
M9B 6E4
(TA)

OAK INDUSTRIES INC.
PO Box 517
Crystal Lake, IL 60014
(EP)

**OFFICIAL AIRLINE GUIDES
INC.**
888 7th Ave.
New York, NY 10106
(IP)

**Key: CS—Cable System; EP—Equipment Provider; IP—Information
Provider; O—Other; SO—System Operator; TA—Telecommunications
Authority; TV—Television Station.**

**ONTARIO EDUCATIONAL
AND COMMUNICATIONS
AUTHORITY**
PO Box 200, Station Q
Toronto, Ontario
M4T 2T1 Canada
(TV)

PANASONIC CO.
**(Division of Matsushita
Electric Corp. of America)**
One Panasonic Way
Secaucus, NJ 07094
(EP)

PHILIPS INDUSTRIES
City House
420-430 London Rd. W.
Croydon CR9 3QR, England
(EP)

PHOENIX NEWSPAPERS INC.
120 East Van Buren St.
Phoenix, AZ 85004
(IP)

PRESTEL HEADQUARTERS
British Telecommunications
Telephone House
Temple Ave.
London EC4Y 0HL, England
(SO, TA)

**PUBLIC BROADCASTING
SERVICE (PBS)**
475 L'Enfant Plaza SW
Washington, DC 20024
(TV)

PYE LTD.
137 Ditton Walk
Cambridge CB5 8QD, England
(EP)

RADIO BROADCASTING CO.
3600 Conshohocken Ave.
Philadelphia, PA 19131
(TV)

**RADIO RENTALS CON-
TRACTS LTD.**
Apex House
Twickenham Rd.
Feltham TW13 6JQ, England
(EP)

RADIO SHACK
385 5th Ave.
New York, NY 10016
(EP)

**RADOFIN ELECTRONICS
LTD.**
10b Engelhard Ave.
Avenel, NJ 07001
(EP)

**RANK RADIO INTER-
NATIONAL**
Northolt Ave., Ernsettle
Plymouth, Devon PL5 2TS
England
(EP)

**RCA MICROCOMPUTER
PRODUCTS**
New Holland Ave.
Lancaster, PA 17604
(EP)

**Key: CS—Cable System; EP—Equipment Provider; IP—Information
Provider; O—Other; SO—System Operator; TA—Telecommunications
Authority; TV—Television Station.**

REDIFFUSION COMPUTERS LTD.
Kelvin Way
Crawley
W. Sussex RH10 2LY, England
(EP)

REUTERS (NORTH AMERICA)
1700 Broadway
New York, NY 10019
(IP)

SATELLITE SYNDICATED SYSTEMS
8252 South Harvard
Tulsa, OK 74136
(O)

SEARS ROEBUCK & CO.
Sears Tower
Chicago, IL 60684
(IP)

S.E.D. SYSTEMS LTD.
2415 Koyl
Saskatoon, Saskatchewan
Canada
(O)

SOCIOSCOPE INC.
94 Wurtemburg St.
Ottawa, Ontario, Canada
K1N 8M2
(O)

SOFRATEV
21 rue de La Vanne
92120 Montrouge, France
(TV)

SONY CORP. OF AMERICA
9 W. 57th St.
New York, NY 10019
(EP)

SONY (UK)
Pyrene House
Sunbury Cross
Sunbury-on-Thames TW16 7AT
England
(EP)

SOURCE TELECOMPUTING CORP.
1616 Anderson Rd.
McLean, VA 22102
(IP, SO)

SOUTHAM, INC.
321 Bloor E.
Toronto, Ontario, Canada
(IP)

STANDARD TELEPHONES & CABLES
Oakleigh Rd. S.
New Southgate, London N11 1HB
England
(EP)

SVERIGES RADIO
Oxenstiernsgatan 20
S-105
101 Stockholm, Sweden
(TV)

Key: CS—Cable System; EP—Equipment Provider; IP—Information Provider; O—Other; SO—System Operator; TA—Telecommunications Authority; TV—Television Station.

SYSTEMHOUSE LTD.
99 Bank St.
Ottawa, Ontario, Canada
K1P 6B9
(EP)

TANDY CORP.
RADIO SHACK
1600 One Tandy Ctr.
Fort Worth, TX 76102
(EP)

TDF (Telediffusion de France)
2127 Rue Barbes
Montrouge 92100, France
(TV)

TECHNALOGICS COM-PUTING LTD.
394 Scotland Rd.
Taylor Street Ind. Est
Liverpool L5 5AD, England
(O)

TELECABLE VIDEOTRON
37 Losch Blvd.
St-Hubert, Quebec, Canada
J3Y 5T6
(CS)

TELE-COMMUNICATIONS INC.
54 Denver Technological Ctr.
Denver, CO 80210
(CS)

TELEFUSION LTD.
Telefusion House
Preston New Rd.
Blackpool FY4 4QY, England
(EP)

TELEPROMPTER CORP.
(now called Group W Cable)
See Westinghouse Broadcasting
& Cable, Inc.

TELIC ALCATEL
102 rue du Point de Jour
92100 Boulogne, France
(EP)

TELIDON CORP.
3 Landmark Sq.
Suite 400
Stamford, CT 06901
(O)

TELIDON MARKETING SECRETARIAT, DEPT. OF INDUSTRY, TRADE & COMMERCE
107 Sparks St.
4th Floor
Ottawa K1A 0H5, Canada
(O)

TEXAS INSTRUMENTS
PO Box 2474
Dallas, TX 75222
(EP)

Key: CS—Cable System; EP—Equipment Provider; IP—Information Provider; O—Other; SO—System Operator; TA—Telecommunications Authority; TV—Television Station.

THOMSON-CSF DRT
146 Boulevard de Valmy
92707 Colombes Cedex, France
(EP)

**THORN CONSUMER ELEC-
TRONICS LTD.**
Thorn House
Upper St. Martin's La.
London WC2, England
(EP)

TIME INC.
Time & Life Bldg.
New York, NY 10020
(CS, IP, SO)

**TIMES MIRROR VIDEOTEX
SERVICES**
1375 Sunflower Ave.
Costa Mesa, CA 92626
(IP, SO)

TORSTAR CORP.
1 Yonge St.
Toronto, Ontario, Canada
M5E1P9
(IP)

**TV ONTARIO, TELIDON PRO-
JECT**
PO Box 200, Sta. Q
Toronto, Ontario, Canada
M4T 2T1
(TV)

TYMSHARE INC.
20705 Valley Green Dr.
Cupertino, CA 95014
(EP, SO)

**UNITED MEDIA ENTER-
PRISE**
200 Park Ave.
New York, NY 10166
(IP)

**UNITED PRESS INTER-
NATIONAL**
220 E. 42nd St.
New York, NY 10017
(IP)

**UNIVERSAL PRESS
SYNDICATE**
1271 Ave. of the Americas
Suite 3717
New York, NY 10020
(IP)

**VIACOM INTERNATIONAL
INC.**
1211 6th Ave.
New York, NY 10036
(CS, TV)

VIDEODIAL
15 Columbus Circle
New York, NY 10023
(EP, O)

VIDEOTEX AMERICA
1381 Morse Ave.
Irvine, CA 92714
(O)

**Key: CS—Cable System; EP—Equipment Provider; IP—Information
Provider; O—Other; SO—System Operator; TA—Telecommunications
Authority; TV—Television Station.**

**VIDEOTEX INDUSTRY
ASSOCIATION**
2000 L St. NW
Washington, DC 20036
(O)

**VIEWDATA CORP. OF
AMERICA, INC.**
1111 Lincoln Rd.
Miami, FL 33139
(IP, SO)

VIEWTEL SERVICES LTD.
28 Colmore Circus
Queensway
Birmingham B4 6AX, England
(IP)

WALDENBOOKS
201 High Ridge Rd.
Stamford, CT 06904
(IP)

**WARNER COMMUNI-
CATIONS INC.**
10 Rockefeller Plaza
New York, NY 10020
(CS, IP)

WESTERN ELECTRIC CO.
222 Broadway
New York, NY 10038
(EP)

**WESTINGHOUSE BROAD-
CASTING & CABLE, INC.**
888 7th Ave.
New York, NY 10106
(CS, TV)

WETA-TV
Box 2626
Washington, DC 20013
(TV)

WFLD-TV
Marina City
300 N. State St.
Chicago, IL 60610
(TV)

WGBH-TV
125 Western Ave.
Boston, MA 02134
(TV)

WKRC-TV
1906 Highland Ave.
Cincinnati, OH 45219
(TV)

WTBS-TV
1018 W. Peachtree St.
Atlanta, GA 30309
(TV)

ZENITH RADIO CORP.
1000 N. Milwaukee Ave.
Glenview, IL 60025
(EP)

**Key: CS—Cable System; EP—Equipment Provider; IP—Information
Provider; O—Other; SO—System Operator; TA—Telecommunications
Authority; TV—Television Station.**

Bibliography: For Further Reference

BOOKS AND REPORTS

Fedida, Sam and Rex Malik. *The Viewdata Revolution*. New York: John Wiley and Sons, 1979.

Larratt, Richard, editor. *Inside Videotex: The Future... Now*. Proceedings of a seminar held March 13-14, 1980. Toronto, Canada: Infomart, 1980.

Martin, James. *The Wired Society: A Challenge for Tomorrow*. Englewood Cliffs: Prentice-Hall, Inc., 1978.

Neustadt, Richard. *The Birth of Electronic Publishing: Legal and Economic Issues in Telephone, Cable and Over-the-Air Teletext and Videotext*. White Plains: Knowledge Industry Publications, Inc., 1982.

Sigel, Efrem, editor. *Videotext: The Coming Revolution in Home/Office Information Retrieval*. White Plains: Knowledge Industry Publications, Inc., 1980.

Smith, Anthony. *Goodbye Gutenberg: The Newspaper Revolution of the 1980s*. New York: Oxford University Press, 1980.

Spigai, Fran and Peter Sommer. *Guide to Electronic Publishing: Opportunities in Online and Viewdata Services*. White Plains: Knowledge Industry Publications, Inc., 1982.

Tydeman, John, et al. *Teletext and Videotext in the United States: Market Potential, Technology, Public Policy Issues*. Menlo Park: Institute for the Future, March 1982.

Videotex '81 International Conference & Exhibition, May 20-22, 1981, Proceedings. Middlesex, UK: Online Conferences Ltd., 1981.

Videotext—key to the information revolution. Middlesex, UK: Online Publications, Ltd., 1982.

Viewdata and Videotext, 1980-81: A Worldwide Report. Transcript of Viewdata '80. White Plains: Knowledge Industry Publications, Inc., 1980.

PERIODICALS

Advertising Age (Crain Communications Inc., Chicago, IL)
Broadcasting (Broadcasting Publications Inc., Washington, DC)
Cablevision (Titsch Communications, Inc., Denver, CO)
Communications News (Harcourt Brace Jovanovitch, Inc., Geneva, IL)
Computer Business News (C.W. Communications, Inc., Newton, MA)
Computerworld (C.W. Communications, Inc., Framingham, MA)
Data Communications (McGraw-Hill Publications Co., New York, NY)
Datamation (Technical Publishing, Barrington, IL)
Education & Industrial Television (C.S. Tepfer Publishing Company, Inc., Danbury, CT)
Electronics (McGraw-Hill Publications Co., New York, NY)
Home Video and Cable Report (Knowledge Industry Publications, Inc., White Plains, NY)
Information and Data Base Publishing Report (Knowledge Industry Publications, Inc., White Plains, NY)
Intermedia (International Institute of Communications, London, UK)
International Videotex/Teletext News (Arlen Communications, Inc., Bethesda, MD)
Journal of Broadcasting (Broadcast Education Association, University of Georgia, Athens, GA)
Journal of Communication (The Annenberg School Press, University of Pennsylvania, Philadelphia, PA)
MIS Week (Fairchild Publications, New York, NY)
The Pay TV Newsletter (Paul Kagan Associates, Carmel, CA)
Public Telecommunications Review (National Association of Educational Broadcasters, Washington, DC)
Telecommunications Policy (IPC Business Press, Ltd., New York, NY)
Telephony (Telephony Publishing Corp., Chicago, IL)
Television Digest (Television Digest, Inc., Washington, DC)
Television/Radio Age (Television Editorial Corp., Easton, PA)
Videodisc/Videotex (Meckler Publishing, Westport, CT)

Index

About the Authors

Efrem Sigel is president and publisher of Communications Trends, Inc. He is editor and co-author of *Videotext: The Coming Revolution in Home/Office Information Retrieval* and co-author of *Video Discs: The Technology, the Applications and the Future*; *Books, Libraries and Electronics: Essays on the Future of Written Communication* and *Crisis! The Taxpayer Revolt and Your Kids' Schools*. He is also author of *The Kermanshah Transfer*, a novel. Mr. Sigel is a graduate of Harvard College and the Harvard University Graduate School of Business Administration.

Peter Sommer has worked for Harrap Books and Granada Publishing where he became Deputy Editorial Director. He was also viewdata consultant for *Practical Computing* magazine. In 1980, Mr. Sommer set up a Prestel information provider company, LOTC, which publishes information on British over-the-counter securities. In June 1981 he joined AVS Intext, one of the largest Prestel information providers, as senior consultant. Author of a number of educational and other nonfiction books, Mr. Sommer has also written for such publications as *The Observer* and *Time Out*, and is co-author of *Guide to Electronic Publishing: Opportunities in Online and Viewdata Services*.

Jeffrey Silverstein is managing editor of *IDP Report*, a twice monthly newsletter covering online information publishing and videotext industries, and associate editor of the *Home Video and Cable Report*, a weekly newsletter, both published by Knowledge Industry Publications, Inc. Previously, Mr. Silverstein, a graduate of Colgate University, was a newspaper reporter and freelance writer.

Colin McIntyre was the first journalist to participate in the development of the BBC's teletext service and was editor of CEEFAX from 1974 to 1982. He had been associated with the BBC since 1952, where his positions have included United Nations correspondent, chief publicity officer and Programme Promotions Executive. Mr. McIntyre is a graduate of Harvard University and the Open University and is presently a freelance teletext consultant. He contributed to *Videotext: The Coming Revolution in Home/Office Information Retrieval*.

Blaise Downey is a freelance journalist based in Ottawa, Canada. His articles on high technology industry have appeared in a variety of technical, trade and government publications. Mr. Downey has lived in Canada since 1957 after graduating from university in his native Dublin, Ireland.